Praise for *Pure*

Mike Thiessen has written an uncommonly common-sense book on male-female relationships that honors and celebrates God's distinctive design for marriage between a complementary man and woman. Using accessible, real-world experiences and the truth of Scripture, he treats the subject of marriage and sex with the warmth and dignity it rightly deserves.

REV. JOE BOOT, SENIOR PASTOR, WESTMINSTER CHAPEL, TORONTO; FOUNDER OF THE EZRA INSTITUTE FOR CONTEMPORARY CHRISTIANITY; AUTHOR OF *THE MISSION OF GOD: A MANIFESTO OF HOPE*

In a culture in which instant-sexual-gratification-without-commitment is promoted as the pinnacle of human happiness, *Pursuing a First-Class Marriage* helps young adults (and the parents who love them) think through questions about dating and relationships in an authentically Christian way. Honest, wise, and practical, Michael Thiessen is not afraid of tackling the difficult questions head-on and as he does, offers a beautiful and biblical vision of what marriage can really be.

DR. ANDY BANNISTER, DIRECTOR AND LEAD APOLOGIST, RZIM CANADA; AUTHOR OF *THE ATHEIST WHO DIDN'T EXIST*

Followers of Jesus Christ are called to resist conformity to the wider culture, and nowhere is this more crucial than in the area of dating, courtship, and marriage. All around us, Christians are failing in the area of sexual ethics. But perhaps the greater problem is the failure of pastors and teachers to talk candidly about sex. In this book, Mike Thiessen helps us think biblically and realistically about the way we move toward marriage. The book is true both to Scripture and to the realities of human experience. I hope this book will help people who are headed toward marriage, and stimulate pastors to talk about the topic courageously.

DR. STAN K. FOWLER, PROFESSOR OF THEOLOGICAL STUDIES, HERITAGE COLLEGE AND SEMINARY; AUTHOR OF *RETHINKING BAPTISM: SOME BAPTIST REFLECTIONS*

Michael Thiessen has provided us with a refreshing and thoroughly biblical alternative to our sexually supercharged culture. Michael helps us rethink dating, marriage, sexuality, and commitment by taking us to God's blueprint and illustrating his themes in a creative manner through the image of flight. If you are a church leader, an educator, a parent, or a person who thinks you are ready for a relationship, this promises to be an important read.

Dr. Michael Pawelke, president, Briercrest College and Seminary; author of Disciple: A Catalyst to Transformation

To a culture that promotes variety over value, tinkering over thinking, and fun over faithfulness, *Pursuing a First-Class Marriage* offers a biblical trajectory for navigating the often turbulent process of finding "the one." Michael Thiessen simultaneously entertains and instructs, making this book an ideal gift for high school graduates and college students.

Dr. Mark Scott, assistant professor, Thorneloe University; author of Pathways in Theodicy: An Introduction to the Problem of Evil

Mike Thiessen provides an easy-to-read, easy-to-understand book on the biblical view of marriage. But that doesn't mean Mike shies away from the more difficult and delicate issues in contemporary culture. Not at all; Mike deals with pertinent and meaningful facets of twenty-first-century courtship and marriage by carefully examining biblical truth, applying it to current trends, and expressing it in a thoughtful and sensitive manner.

Randall Spacht, international church development, One Mission Society

Pursuing a First-Class Marriage

PURSUING A First-Class Marriage

FIND THE ONE WITHOUT TRYING MANY

With love in Christ,

Michael Thiessen

Deep River
BOOKS

Pursuing a First-Class Marriage
Published by Deep River Books
© 2016 by Michael Thiessen

All Scripture quotations, unless otherwise indicated, are taken from *The Holy Bible, New International Version*. NIV. © 1973, 1978, 1984 by International Bible Society. Used by permission of Zondervan Publishing House.

Scripture quotations marked "ESV" are taken from *The Holy Bible: English Standard Version*. © 2001 by Crossway. Used by permission of Good News Publishers.

All rights reserved. No part of this publication may be reproduced, stored in a retrieval system, or transmitted in any form or by any means—electronic, mechanical, photocopy, recording, or any other—except for brief quotations in printed reviews or classroom settings, without the prior permission of the publisher.

ISBN: 9781940269740

Library of Congress: 2015955931

Cover design by Robin Black, Inspirio Design

Published in the USA

To Sarah, my Princess:

YOU'VE STOLEN MY HEART!
MY CHRISTIAN SISTER, MY BRIDE!
YOU'VE STOLEN MY HEART!
WITH ONE GLANCE OF YOUR EYES!

To my children, Simon and Gabriel,
Maylah-Belle and Galilee-Ling:

HOW CAN A YOUNG ONE KEEP THE WAY PURE?
BY LIVING ACCORDING TO GOD'S WORD!

---

*To the young woman who longs to find companionship
with a man who will stay faithful;
To the young man who is driven to find sex and friendship
with a woman who will be devoted:*

WAIT! SLOW DOWN! THINK!
THE FEAR OF THE LORD IS THE BEGINNING OF KNOWLEDGE.

CONTENTS

    Acknowledgments 11

    Introduction 13

1. Check-In 17
2. Security Gate A: Truth Exists 29
3. Security Gate B: Trust Christ 37
4. Security Gate C: Why Friends Become Lovers 53
5. Boarding and Departure 77
6. In-flight Lounging 95
7. Baggage Claims 125
8. Arrival 139

    Endnotes 163

Acknowledgments

The writing process is a humbling experience. It is so easy to overstate or over-simplify ideas. I often need help with my tone and nuancing because I tend to be bombastic. I am preacher by trade, after all. Many individuals have taken the time to read early versions of this work. These editors have added so much to the book. They have given me valuable feedback and direction.

First, I am so thankful for Alexandra Nahl, who acted as an early editor within my target audience. Her comments and edits as a young woman were tremendously helpful to my manuscript. I appreciated her encouraging feedback and criticisms. She allowed me to hear her voice in my head saying, "Are you sure about that?" She remained engaged and detailed in her editorial work, even though she disagreed with my worldview at times.

Second, I am thankful for friends such as Lori Horner and Jenn Birnie, who helped sharpen some of my sections about friendship. Dr. Mark Scott provided much encouragement for me to stick it out. After many calls and questions, he continued to say, "Refine, refine, refine."

Third, I wish to thank my editor at Deep River Books, Mark Weising. Mark simplified my prose and subtitles. The flow and tone of the book became much better through Mark's revisions. I am indebted to his clear sequential thoughts.

Finally, my life is on these pages. That means my wife and children have let the readers into their lives too. I am grateful to my wife, Sarah, who has given me support throughout the project and allowed me to be vulnerable concerning our personal stories and short-fallings. Sarah's thoughts enrich this text. And, as I don't have everything together, either as a husband, father, pastor, and now author, Sarah walks with me, enduring the pressure that builds while ministering in a glass house before others and giving me daily grace. My children often endure having their lives opened before others. This is no exception. I am thankful for them loving me, even though I don't always practice what I preach. I love you Simon, Gabriel, Maylah-Belle, and Galilee-Ling.

Introduction

As a pastor, I am constantly asked the same questions by young adults. Guys want to know how a girl could spend so much time with them and just want to be friends. Girls want to know why guys are always looking for more and are not content with just being friends. Guys want to know what girls really want from them, and girls want to know what guys really want from them. I hear many other questions as well, such as:

- What's so wrong with "hooking up"? What could I possibly lose if I have sex before marriage? What could I gain if I wait to have sex until after marriage?
- Shouldn't I have sex right away with someone I like so I know if we're sexually compatible?
- Don't I need to be "sexually experienced" so I can perform well in marriage?
- What's wrong with living together? Isn't it the best way to see if I and the other person should be together?
- How do I know when I've found the one?

Parents also ask me lots of questions. They want to know:

- What responsibility do I have in my child finding a spouse?
- When should I let my son or daughter date?
- How can I set boundaries for them without driving them away?
- How do I talk to them about sex and dating in a meaningful and persuasive way?

This book is my response to these questions. While it is not written for Christians only, it is written *by* a Christian. I believe with my whole heart that "God so loved the world that he gave his one and only Son, that whoever believes in him shall not perish but have eternal life" (John 3:16).

I once sat in a room feeling lost. I was in the party scene and drinking regularly, even though I would always feel awful the next day. I would often steal, even though my parents took great care of me and I had already been caught as a young offender. And I was intensely lonely, even though I was surrounded by people. I longed so much for a deep friendship with a woman that also included romance.

One night, I prayed to God for help. "God," I said, "if you really exist, help me get out of this mess, and help me find my future wife who will help me to be stronger." God answered the first part of this prayer by forcing me out of the party scene. Within two days, my employment circumstances changed, which caused me to move cities for other employment. I was out and away from it all. I moved back into my parents' home for one summer—and that summer changed my life. God then helped me find the woman who would become my wife. I went to college and established a great friendship with a girl named Sarah. She befriended me and has loved me, been committed to me, helped me, and sharpened me ever since.

If you've picked up this book and don't share my faith, know that I will be speaking a lot about both Jesus and the Bible. But please don't put the book down right now because of that. Stay and investigate Jesus for a while. Permit yourself to consider what Christ might teach you.

I began writing with you in mind as I sat in my son's hospital room. He was diagnosed with hepatoblastoma while we were living in Southern Africa, so in 2009 we returned to Canada to have him treated at Toronto's Hospital for Sick Children. The outline for this manuscript took shape in that room of the oncology ward. My two-year-old son Gabriel was receiving chemotherapy through a port in his chest and was sleeping soundly in his bed.

As I sat there, taking the night shift, I began to reflect about our cancer experience. I remembered how many times my wife, Sarah, and I would say to each other, "I can't imagine going through this without you." We meant it from the depths of our hearts, and I realized at that moment how thankful I was for my marriage. I also realized I had to set something down on paper to guide young adults on their own journeys toward marriage.

Many young people today don't know what to avoid when it comes to relationships. Some have a negative or incomplete view of marriage, and others don't know how to deal with sexual aggression. Many expect to just "fall" in love, and some hold back on pursuing relationships to follow other endeavors. I am concerned for these young people. Sarah and I are so thankful that our marriage continues to develop and that our friendship grows stronger each day because of the teachings of Christ. I want to share His truth with others.

If you are a Christian young person entering into this journey, I want to thank you for honoring me with your time and your mind. I hope in the years to come we will see a resurgence of happy marriages, blissful friendships, and healthy families in the church. As you are looking for a pure spouse, don't be hasty. Consider what steps to take. Let the thoughts here develop. Percolate on them like coffee brewing. When you are startled or confronted, reflect, jot down some questions, and then read on to see what I truly mean.

Remember that sex can be impure if you joke about it, mistreat its language, and disrespect the opposite gender. Keep your eyes on the prize of purity and maturity while I discuss some pretty intense and personal things. I hope you see something of beauty by the end. I see it. It hangs like a work of art on the wall of an airport in the arrival area. It's gilded with golden love and is forged in the fires of struggle and refinement. It reflects the rich colors of commitment, trust, and sacrifice. It's bright and brilliant.

If you are a parent of a young adult who will be entering this journey, please be intentional as you guide your child into adulthood. Read this book first. Read ahead. Read along with your child. Some things are going to sound seventeenth-century to you, but don't default to our culture's norms and secular dating habits. It is time to call your sons and daughters back from the cliff. Other things you read are going to make you blush. You're going to squirm as your child reads about sex, but I will keep my dialogue wholesome and pure. Our culture melts conversations about sexuality into warm butter to make it unclear and messy. I want to cut through that like a knife, quick and decisive.

I hope these thoughts help you target your child toward Christlike living. I hope you get serious about talking to your teens and college students about marriage. Too many parents are apathetic and distant from their own experiences and failures as young adults. Know that just because you did something one way—maybe the hard, foolish, gathering-baggage way—you don't need to project your failures onto your kids. Be mindful enough to know them, be generous enough to love them, and be brave enough to lead them.

One
CHECK-IN

GETTING READY TO FLY

When we're young, life is like walking toward a new sun rising! It's rock concerts! Life when we're young is an adventurous journey. It's flying for the first time. For this reason, I want to compare dating to an airline flight. When we travel, we're all so excited to meet new people and arrive at a pristine, interesting, and life-changing destination. The same is true of courtship. The goal is to arrive at marriage while having a safe and mindful journey along the way.

I like to watch the English Premiere League. I believe it's the toughest and most aggressive expression of the "world game," which we in North America know as soccer. It's brilliant! I love it! However, living across the ocean makes it difficult for me to see my favorite English team play. I can't get into any old plane and fly in any old direction to get across to Old Trafford, one of England's most historic football stadiums. The same is true for you. You can't just ask one of your friends to catch a derby and—*poof!*—you're there. I assure you London will be inspiring, the stands will be roaring, the pitch will be perfect, and the teams will be top notch. I assure you the ball will be struck and the goals will be immaculate. But there is a *process* to getting there. There are things you simply must do.

I am equally excited by happy marriages. Not many people desire the single life. God made most of us with the drive to join together and produce children. We see this in our biology, as our parts fit together. We feel this in our longings, as the majority of us yearn for a relationship that brings oneness out of twoness. I love it when a man and a woman thrive together in friendship and intimacy. I love to see children laughing, growing up with both parents, and experiencing disciplined and joyful love.

In my mind, marriage is one of the most worthwhile adventures in life.

It is magnificent to see a home full of love, respect, and dedication. As parents are faithful to one another, one generation passes on goodness and godliness to the next—and we all know the world needs more goodness to be passed on! We don't want just fluff and empty promises. We need substantive, meaty, twelve-ounce-steak-goodness to be modeled and exhibited in family life. However, just like traveling overseas for a soccer match, there is a *process* to getting there. There are things we must do to prepare for a great marriage.

Personally, I always wanted to be married young. My goal was to choose a great female friend, have lots of sex, travel the globe, eat good food, and live out our shared passion for Jesus by doing something that changed the world. However, like so many others, I took my eyes off that target when I become a young adult. During my teenage years, I pursued about four girls seriously. In each case we became friends, and then I became interested in being more than friends. I dated two of the girls and resolved to be just friends with the others.

At some points I was rejected and at other points I did the rejecting. It hurt in each situation. I continue even now to lament the awkwardness of that stage of life. I eventually gave up pursuing a "girlfriend" and just messed around with girls at parties. I held back, but not enough to be pure. I was strongly tempted to pass through the doorway of sexual intercourse. Yet one friend helped at a particular moment by confronting me and saying, "No, in your heart you know that you don't want to cross that line."

If you are anticipating the joy of a future relationship and want to know what will make it flourish and last, take some advice from a friend who is ahead in the journey. Sarah and I were married very young. Many people mocked our commitment as being idealistic, premature, and inexperienced. However, the day Sarah accepted my marriage proposal was one of the most fulfilling days of my life. I had never experienced complete acceptance and commitment like that before. My beautiful Sarah continues to be faithful to me. She accepts my invitation to journey beside me. She chooses to stand with me, to lie down with me, and to walk the road with me. Now and forever, I want to honor her, love her, protect her, and finish the good thing we've started.

I want the same for you. I want you to find the one who will remain faithful to you. But, as I've said, there are some things that both of you will have to do.

THERE'S NOTHING CASUAL ABOUT IT

The romantic comedy *When Harry Met Sally* was released in 1989, when I was thirteen years old. I saw the movie three or four years later with my two older sisters. Being the youngest of three, and the only boy, I ended up watching more romantic comedies than I'd like to admit. However, something clicked for me that night as a seventeen-year-old. The main theme of the movie is simple: *a great relationship must include friendship, commitment, and then sex. Casually hooking-up just creates pain and problems.*

Now, to be honest, you have to look for this in the film. You have to wait for it. Writers love to complicate the plot and frustrate the audience with tension. Because of this, the message is never explicitly stated, and the characters have to clumsily find it at the end.

Since the time *When Harry Met Sally* came out, numerous reboots on the same idea have emerged. TV sitcoms like *Friends, 90210,* and *The Big Bang Theory,* along with movies like *Friends with Benefits* and *No Strings Attached,* have each created its own twist on the friendship dilemma. Characters are always looking for a spouse but never finding one among their friends. They are always seeking permanent love but are always settling on hasty temporary sex. In the end the writers have to resolve the tension of casual dating, and they do so with the same age-old solution: *Great relationships include friendship, commitment, and then sex.*

Even though *When Met Harry and Sally* is becoming a bit outdated, I still believe it combines a brilliant theme with a powerful message. Let me paint the context a bit.

Scene 1: The Question Is Posed

Harry and Sally meet when they decide to carpool home from college together. Harry is dating one of Sally's friends, but he seems somewhat attracted to Sally. He confirms our suspicions when he tells her she's attractive.

She takes it as a pickup line. Her response, personifying most women, is, "we'll just be friends."

Pause button…

Now, I believe this is a defining and universal value for women when they enter into relationships with men. I will attempt to show you, based on Scripture and study, that women find deep satisfaction in relationships that are based on close friendships. Even though women have hopes for sex, and even though there may be exceptions, friendship is a feminine default relationship setting. It is of first importance to them. They expect it to be as natural for us men.

When I use the term "friend," I mean people who are more than acquaintances. We all have people with whom we are friendly, but when I speak about friendship, I mean someone with whom we spend time one-on-one to build greater connections. We all have group friends and go on group outings as a mob. I am not talking about this nuance of friendship. Rather, I am making the definition more specific to limit its meaning and application.

FRIENDSHIP: *a state of mutual trust and ongoing support; a person with whom one has a bond of mutual affection.*

Let's continue with the scene from *When Harry Met Sally*. Harry's response to Sally, personifying most men, is, "Men and women can't be friends, because the sex part always gets in the way."

Pause button…

Now, I believe this is a defining and universal drive for men as they enter into relationships with women. I will attempt to show you, based on Scripture and study, that men find deep satisfaction in relationships that are built on friendship and sex. We value sex so much that we can't separate the two for long. Sex is a masculine default relationship setting. It is of first importance to us. We expect it to be as natural for women.

Guys, we should all be smirking at this. We *know* we move way too fast.

I was out fishing on Lake Simcoe the other day, which is just north of

Toronto. I rarely fish, and I'm not any good at it. However, I have a buddy who makes it fun, and we have another buddy who makes us laugh a lot. So I was out fishing, sitting around talking to my married buddies, and we got laughing about sex. One of my friends said, "When guys are with their wives, they think, 'Hey, we're alone. Let's get naked and have some fun. It will kick the fun factor up a notch. Vacuuming can wait, or it too can be done naked.'" We all knew exactly what he meant. We value sex. It is our default setting.

SCENES 2–14: THE TENSION BUILDS

Sally takes offence to Harry's statement about sex. She asserts, "I have lots of friends who are men." Throughout the movie, the audience is left to find out who is right. Is it Harry? Or is it Sally? The audience wants to know if men and women can just be friends without having sex. Women want to know if men really do care that much about having sex. When will he stop being such a pig and just care for her and talk with her? Men want to know if women really do care that much about being friends. When will she see he is dying to be fully accepted by her?

THE FINALE: THE QUESTION IS ANSWERED

Harry and Sally battle against the obnoxious and obvious conclusion that friendship attraction really does exist. In one sense they already understand it, but they continue to fight its existence. In the end, they finally see that both their impulses—women for friendship and men for sex—must be fulfilled for them to stay together. Moreover, they discover these desires are most naturally fulfilled in an old mysterious thing called "marriage," which incorporates pleasure for both individuals by meeting the needs of both individuals.

Harry finds out that sex without friendship is completely empty. He sees that all of the women in his past who he rushed to sleep with didn't make him happy. He finds himself standing alone on New Year's Eve, thinking about companionship—forever lasting, wonderfully jealous, "I don't want anyone else to be best friends with her" companionship.

Sally finds out that friendships with men don't last if intimacy isn't involved. She sees that she never remains "just friends" with any of the men in her life—she is always in a relationship. She also fails to remain "just friends" with Harry in their friendship. During the main part of the film, the two become drawn to each other physically. She gets jealous if he's with someone else. She wants love from him and wants a family as well. She, too, finds herself standing alone on New Year's Eve, thinking about companionship—forever lasting, wonderfully jealous, "I don't want anyone else to be intimate with him, ever" companionship.

So…it's New Year's Eve, and Harry realizes how much he loves her. He runs to the party where she is and tells her about all the small personal details he loves about her. She loves that. They rush into each other's arms. They kiss. And they comment on the song playing because they don't know what it's about. She says, "It's about old friends." They kiss again. And we all sigh in relief because "they live happily ever after."

THREE MAIN THEMES

In a future chapter, we will answer the film's question about the relationship between friendship and sex in greater detail. In this chapter, I want to focus on the three themes presented in the movie's conclusion: *friendship*, *sex*, and *commitment*, the last of which creeps in to resolve all the last-minute tension. Let's look at each of these themes.

Friendship

It is obvious within the context of the story that Harry and Sally will continue to be great friends. They grew to love each other through visits to the museum, changing menu orders, and long walks, and the audience assumes they will continue to share meals and talk through life. Harry actually learned to listen to Sally. Even more, he realized he *enjoyed* listening to her and processing with her. It's hard work for guys, but the end result was a great joy. Relationships need this bond of emotional and experiential connection. Distance is not an option.

Sex

It is also clear that Harry and Sally were going home that night to have sex.

They had already moved past the "just friends" idea and had realized the notion was empty and incomplete. Something was missing. In the romantic moment of New Year's Eve, with just a little bit of champagne to brighten their smiles, they were going to start a life of intimacy together. Married couples share this with each other—the physical connection of skin to skin, touch to touch, mouth to mouth. It is real. It is good. It is bliss. In the security of companionship, Sally wanted to give herself to this man. In the coming years of their relationship, as they worked at it, sex would be a beautiful connection point for them.

COMMITMENT

In Harry's final plea, he says to Sally, "When you realize that you want to spend the rest of your life with someone, you want 'the rest of your life' to start as soon as possible." This final plea for happiness comes as a plea for commitment. There is something strangely wonderful in the words "the rest of your life." It solidifies everything. It becomes one of the three things we assume will exist in their relationship from that moment forward.

And Harry and Sally *needed* to be committed to each other forever. They were no longer confused and immature. They had grown up, and this resulted in commitment. The assumption is they would get married just like their other friends who found happiness in marriage. The end game was not just a late-night conversation or a night of passion but a lasting joy shaped by hard work and a lifelong commitment to each other.

FALSE ADVERTISING

For many people, talking about commitment and purity in this way poses a problem. After all, it confronts popular attitudes toward sexuality and global habits of dating, both of which suggest people should try many partners before they choose one spouse. In Tracy Clark-Flory's article "In Defense of Casual Sex," she provides a perfect example of this "hookup" or "taste and see" attitude so prominent in our culture:

> I lost my virginity at sixteen with my first love and best friend; it was all champagne and roses.... [Then] there was the cartoonist.

The first night we hooked up, he took me back to his house and played guitar, sang every song he'd ever written, and juggled his collection of vitamin pill bottles.... Then there was the lawyer. We would have passionate, hours-long debates, as though we were opposing counsels in court.... Then there was the pilot, whom I would see whenever his flight schedule brought him in town.... As far as I can tell, these choices don't form a pattern, *other than a refusal to really choose*.... In a few cases, I felt used, but other times I felt like the user.... There's nothing unusual about my experience...I learned something from all of the men I dated...[and] hopefully, by taking several test-drives before buying, we'll be happier with our final investment.[1]

This attitude is so socially accepted that today seventy-seven percent of young adults will have premarital sex by age twenty and more than ninety-one percent will have premarital sex by age thirty.[2] People seem to believe the propaganda that we should "taste and see" before choosing, which means many relationships today are just empty talk and casual-physical playing around. *There is a refusal to really choose,* and so "being together" has little to no meaning because it doesn't communicate any sort of commitment. However, the idea that we may eventually find true satisfaction after trying many different people is false advertising. People are not cars. If we take them for test drives, we damage them.

CHECK IN

Whether male or female, if we are finding instant gratification through casual physical encounters or borderless relationships, we need to become more thoughtful about commitment. We need to stand back and evaluate ourselves for a few minutes. We can't be deceived—instant gratification doesn't last. We must "check in" our minds. Jesus actually let a friend *die* to teach us this lesson:

> Now a man named Lazarus was sick. He was from Bethany, the village of Mary and her sister Martha. (This Mary, whose brother

Lazarus now lay sick, was the same one who poured perfume on the Lord and wiped his feet with her hair.) So the sisters sent word to Jesus, "Lord, the one you love is sick."...Jesus loved Martha and her sister and Lazarus. So when he heard that Lazarus was sick, he stayed where he was two more days.... He went on to tell them, "Our friend Lazarus has fallen asleep; but I am going there to wake him up." His disciples replied, "Lord, if he sleeps, he will get better." Jesus had been speaking of his death, but his disciples thought he meant natural sleep. So then he told them plainly, "Lazarus is dead, and for your sake I am glad I was not there, so that you may believe. But let us go to him now" (John 11:1-3, 5-6, 11-15).

When Jesus was on earth, He was not interested in his friends' instant gratification. He had far better things to teach them. This meant they had to go through painful situations and have patience to see what He was teaching them. In this situation, Jesus demonstrated His power only after He had allowed Lazarus to die. He eventually raised Lazarus from the dead to prove He was sent from God, but Mary, Martha, the disciples, and everyone else had to wait. In this way, He taught them something greater so they would believe in Him.

The message that Lazarus was ill probably took one full day to reach Jesus, for He was staying across the Jordan River about twenty-five kilometers east of Bethany. When the message arrived, Christ made a bold statement that "this sickness will not end in death. No, it is for God's glory so that God's Son may be glorified through it" (John 11:4). This implies that Lazarus was still alive at this point. The sickness hadn't overtaken him yet, even though it soon would. After Christ heard the news, He intentionally waited two days. Only then did He say, "Let us go back to Judea," explaining that "Lazarus is dead."

So the story unfolds when Christ received the message that Lazarus was sick, He supernaturally knew when Lazarus had died sometime after that, and then they all departed for Bethany to fulfill Christ's promise that "this will not end in death." As another day or two was taken up with the return trip, Lazarus stayed in the tomb for at least four days. We know this because at Lazarus' tomb Martha warned Christ, "By this time there is a bad odor, for he has been there four days" (verse 39).

Lazarus died while Christ waited. Lazarus was "dead in the dirt," as they say. Christ would eventually raise him from the dead to teach about His power to resurrect the body, so the disciples would believe in Him, but everyone had to wait for Christ's timing. We see the frustration of this waiting in Martha when she states, "Lord, if you had only been here." She had hoped that Christ would rush to their rescue.

So if Jesus really loved Lazarus and his sisters, why did He delay two more days and put the sisters through the agony of their brother's death? Is He indifferent to human suffering? No. This delay ensured Lazarus had been dead long enough so that no one could misinterpret the miracle as a mere resuscitation.[3] This is a powerful lesson about delayed gratification. Jesus didn't give Mary and Martha what they wanted immediately. He made them wait to be reunited with Lazarus in order to teach all His disciples something greater. Listen how the story finishes:

> Then Jesus said, "Did I not tell you that if you believe, you will see the glory of God?" So they took away the stone. Then Jesus looked up and said, "Father, I thank you that you have heard me.'... When he had said this, Jesus called in a loud voice, 'Lazarus, come out!' The dead man came out, his hands and feet wrapped with strips of linen, and a cloth around his face. Jesus said to them, "Take off the grave clothes and let him go." Therefore many of the Jews who had come to visit Mary, and had seen what Jesus did, believed in him (verses 40-41, 43-45).

Mary, Martha, and Lazarus went through great difficulty and grief to experience the glory of God. They endured loss. They suffered confusion. Their future seemed in jeopardy. However, Jesus allowed them to go through all this so they would witness His power at work. Instead of instantly gratifying their needs, He wanted to teach them something eternal.

The path toward a healthy marriage is a much different example of the way God wants us to endure hardship to see His power at work. We don't always understand why we have to wait for sex, but we do have to wait for it, even though everyone else says otherwise. We don't understand why we have to wait for dating relationships, but we do have to wait for them. Instant gratification doesn't last, but delayed godly gratification does.

If you are not yet married, your job—if you want to have a really great marriage in the future—is to see what others don't see right now. Your job is to invest toward that future relationship now and stay invested in it all through life. Show the young men and women around you that you can wait—that you can delay your desires now so they will be more wonderfully fulfilled in the future.

This will be painful. It will be hard. The world will make you feel foolish for it. But you have to think of your high school and university years as an investment and preparation for marriage. God is not interested in your instant gratification because *He has a better gift to give you*. You can't always get what you want right now. You will have to wait for it.

Even though you don't know your future spouse now, you need to keep yourself pure for that person. It's not good enough to be sorry about this later. After all, it's not good enough for a married man to say, "Sex didn't work out last night, so I went to a prostitute." It's not good enough for a married woman to say, "The conversations at the dinner table are boring, so I'm dating someone else now." In the same way, it's not okay for you to say, "Well, I'm not married yet, so I can do whatever I want with whomever I want."

Know that the other party, your future spouse, will be directly affected by the choices you make today. The apostle Paul said, "All other sins a man commits are outside his body, but he who sins sexually sins against his own body" (Romans 6:18). This means sexual sin is something internal. It affects you biologically and mentally. When you sin sexually, you will carry your sexual and emotional experiences everywhere you go. You will carry internal banks of memories into your next relationship and unpack them there. You will compare your spouse to those in your past: "He listened to me more." "She liked that."

People today are entering into all kinds of sexual and emotional relationships without any thought for their future best friend/lover/spouse.

They are carrying baggage from sexual experiences, past relationships, and hopeless fantasies into their future relationships, which is one of the reasons why so many marriages are dissolving. There are approximately 71,000 divorces each year in Canada alone.[4] More and more people are avoiding marriage because of the fear divorce has created in them since childhood. We all want what Harry and Sally had at the end of the movie, but most of us aren't finding it because we are behaving the way they did at the beginning of the movie.

Girls, the good news is you can find a guy to marry and find a friendship! Guys, you can find a girl to marry and have sex! You can both have it without all the baggage. You can have it and make it last for a lifetime. *A man and a woman can both be greatly fulfilled in a long-lasting relationship when friendship and sex are both present in a lifelong committed marriage.*

Neither men nor women find lasting satisfaction in the cliché "we're just friends," and neither finds satisfaction with one-night-stands. Sex without friendship brings despair, and friendship without sex feels like rejection. However, a relationship started with friendship, sealed with commitment, and then celebrated with sexual intimacy becomes bliss. It is awesome, strong, binding, exciting, courageous, ridiculously joyful, admirable, naked, intimate, passionate, and sweet. It is something on which you can build a family.

If we want the smiles and dances on New Year's Eve, we need to navigate our lives wisely now. Just as we won't get to Jamaica by staggering our way into some small storage compartment in the undercarriage of the plane, we must check in and start the appropriate process to intentionally get somewhere. Purity is the most important factor for our future, which means delaying our gratification. It is a better thing. We are all trying to get somewhere, and it's time for us to check in.

Two
SECURITY GATE A: TRUTH EXISTS

TRUTH PROVIDES DIRECTION

When we begin a journey to a new destination, our first stop after check-in will be at the security gates. These are important checkpoints to prepare us for the flight. Here we find out what we need to discard to move forward. I certainly recognized something I needed to leave behind during one such flight.

Sarah and I had been living in Maputo, Mozambique, when our son Gabriel was diagnosed with cancer. We had been working with One Mission Society to establish a small Bible College when we had to depart suddenly. The summer after our return, I traveled back to Africa to put some business in order. It took me six different flights to go to and from Mozambique. Talk about security checkpoints!

On my way home, I remember flying through Zurich and realizing I still had my Swiss army knife in my carry-on bag. I was on my way to the plane, and it paralyzed me for a second. I wasn't surprised I had made it through the Mozambican customs—let's just say their methods of checking bags are a touch behind those of most international airports. However, I was flabbergasted to think I had already made it through Johannesburg and the checkpoints in Zurich carrying the small weapon I had mindlessly brought on the journey.

In the same way I mindlessly carried my knife through security checkpoints, we can carry dangerous thoughts and ideas around with us through life. We have misconceptions about the way things should be, and these will be dangerous to us if we don't discard them. We are full of falsehoods, and these false pretenses will negatively affect our lives, our love, and our valued relationships.

C.S. Lewis, in his book *Out of the Silent Planet*, describes the effect of this falsehood as being "bent." At one point in the story, a human and an alien are discussing contentment in an attempt to understand one another. The alien character has no understanding of war or sexual promiscuity, because his kind is fully content to share their vegetation with one another and remain monogamous with their wives. The human character can hardly understand this kind of purity, which leads the alien to describe the condition of human beings as that of an alien child who is mentally "having some strange twists."

This is so true about us humans. We are a twisted sort. We are bent in our nature and not straight-lined. We are not true, exact, or even accurate in the way we see the world. Instead of being content to be monogamous, we crave more and more physical pleasure or emotional connection, even when it has negative consequences.

The Bible refers to this "bentness" as sin. Our sinful nature was transferred to all of us when Adam and Eve gained knowledge of good and evil. In Genesis 3:7 we read, "Then the eyes of both of them were opened." Evil twisted our perspective, and now we see things from all angles. Up until that point, humans had only seen the possibilities of good and had been content with it. But because we gained the knowledge of evil by rebelling and eating the fruit, we now crave evil pleasures. We have all been imputed with sin by the first act of disobedience. Now, as each of us chooses to act, we not only crave what is good because we know it but also crave what is evil because we know it too.

This bentness twists our perspectives. It darkens our minds. It creates an internal battle within us as we struggle between choosing what we know to be good and right over what is evil and temporarily pleasurable. We tell lies to ourselves and to others, give excuses, or simply ignore evil. We walk long, falsely-marked, evaporating walkways. However, in Romans 12:2, we are told not to conform any longer to the pattern of this world but to be transformed by the renewing of our minds. We all need to have our minds renewed, transformed, and cleansed. This requires outside help. This requires "security gates" and heart checks.

Maybe we are overly anxious because of our desire to be wealthy. Maybe we hide and hold in anger because of our pride. Maybe we are full of lust and have become fixated on sex. Maybe we rebel against authority because we refuse to honor our father and mother. Maybe we steal because we don't want to work hard. We are not to conform any longer to these evils, for they are the patterns of this world. They are patterns of being twisted and will affect the way we view and act in relationships. Instead, we are to be transformed by the renewing of our mind by filling it with truth.

In life, truth functions the same way as a security gate at an airport. Truth takes away all the dangerous falsehoods we carry around in our minds. Truth straightens our bentness. I am convinced we need to be checked, corrected, and then cleared before taking off into the world of relationships. We must let truth do its work in us to make the flight direct and safe. We must throw out the popular notion that truth doesn't matter.

HARD LIVING WRITTEN ALL OVER THEM

Have you ever noticed that people who are burdened with relationship baggage are often lost ideologically? To have an ideology means you have a system of ideas that guides your life. Those who reject these systems are like thirsty people who walk in concentric circles in the desert chanting, "I can't hear you." It is painful to watch the agony of their burdened and parched bondage, but they won't let go of their ignorance or follow you in a straight line to water. They have hard living written all over them.

It's true, even if it sounds harsh. People who are void of morals and ideological convictions can't understand how to navigate relationships because they have no target or boundaries. They float. Their definitions and expectations move. They want to talk about love, but they don't have anything specific to say about it. This leads to major problems.

John Jefferson Davis, a professor of theology, has applied the same idea to law making. He argues that generalized appeals to justice cannot be divorced from the specifics of law. He suggests we can't speak of justice in the abstract. Rather, there must specific commands, stipulations, and consequences in place for each citizen to give justice real meaning.[1]

The written laws of the land guide us to understand what it means to actually live out "being just." If we make a law that commands, "thou shalt not steal," then it is just for us to leave someone else's property alone. If we break this law, we are choosing to act unjustly toward another person, and the government will punish us for this injustice. Thus, specific law makes specific acts of justice possible.

The same works for love, relationships, and marriage. Just as general appeals to justice become meaningless when the specifics of common law are removed, love becomes meaningless without the specifics of moral ideas. Specific morals and ideas make specific acts of love possible. In other words, we can't speak about love in the abstract. For the word "love" to have meaning we must have specific guidelines for relationships, for love becomes meaningless without the specifics of moral thought and action. The moral specifics make it possible to fulfill the requirements of a specific act of love.

This fact applies to every question people have about finding a spouse and staying faithful, including when they should start dating, whether they should live together before they marry, and how they should treat their spouse. If people don't have specific rules about life, they won't have any specific rules about love, and they won't be able to answer these questions with meaning. They won't know what to say, what to do, or how to make decisions. They won't know how these things should operate. Their expectations and rationale will move. For them, it will be like nailing Jell-O to the wall. Their beliefs are aimless, so their relationships become aimless. Their convictions are shapeless, so their relationships become shapeless. They have no guardrails or painted lines to keep their lives on the road, so their relationships zigzag off it and go over a cliff.

You know these people when you see them. Like the middle-aged man who has just lost everything after having an affair but won't admit to his failure. Instead, he tries desperately to convince his teenage son and the younger executives at his company that he's found a new kind of freedom. He has no moral character and has little true happiness. So he resorts to creating a persona, which is just an empty projection of strength. He is not really thoughtful—he just *pretends* to be thoughtful.

We have to throw out this kind of thinking and the culturally popular mantra that truth doesn't matter. Just as specific law is the bowl in which the soup of freedom sits, moral truth is the bowl in which the soup of relationship success rests. There must be specific commands, stipulations, and consequences for each person to follow.

COURAGE TO ADMIT TRUTH

Let me give you an example of how our society tries to discount truth. A while back I was in a comment conversation on a CBC website. We were having a discussion on abortion policies in Canada, and I was getting many mixed responses to my pro-life comments. So I asked a simple question to the forum: "What does 'compassion' mean?" The responses were all over the map. "What does it matter what we believe?" some of them said. "We can't know these things! Leave ideologies out of this. You are a naive Christian!"

Our definition of compassion will affect our particular policy toward abortion. If we think it is compassionate to save a woman from the psychological trauma of killing an unborn baby, then we will council her to birth the baby, care for him, and give him up for adoption if needed. Even if it means putting her own life on the line, it would better for her to sacrifice her own needs to promote life so she might be able to live with honor and peace of mind. Don't soldiers do this? Don't they put their lives on the line to save the helpless?

Furthermore, if we think it is compassionate to save the unborn because each baby is immediately valuable at conception, then we will again advocate for saving the young one's life. Don't we save other little girls from hunger and starvation? How could we not do those things if we believed each child has value right at the start of life? However, if we don't believe anything about the matter, then we will do nothing at all. In my opinion, this is the wrong course.

Barack Obama showed his lack of moral definitions concerning this exact matter in the events leading up to the U.S. Presidential Elections of November 2008. At one point during a debate in August 2008, he was asked, "At what point is a baby entitled to human rights?" Every human embryo is, by definition, an unborn offspring in the process of development within the womb, and it will develop into a fully-grown human adult unless hindered externally or by sickness. The President of the United States should have acknowledged this, but instead he simply replied, "It's above my pay grade."

Do you see how impossible it is to even dialogue with this kind of answer? The daughter asks, "Should I date when I'm twelve?" Dad replies, "It's above my pay grade." The daughter asks, "Should I have sex when I'm fifteen?" Dad replies, "It's above my pay grade." The daughter asks, "Should I abort the baby?" Dad replies, "It's above my pay grade." It is possible to know the truth about all these things. We just need to be willing to admit it.

CENTER IS THE CENTER

Jacque Derrida, a French philosopher and one of the foremost deconstructionist thinkers of postmodern thought, suggested a "rupture" had occurred at a humanities conference at John's Hopkins University on October 21, 1966. Western thought has historically accepted the world has a center, or reference point, or fixed origin. The function of this center is not only to orient, balance, and organize the world but also to limit "free play," such as human action.

"The center is not the center," Derrida famously said, but rather "a series of substitutions of center for center." In other words, according to Derrida, the limitation of our language and thought inhibits us from knowing anything with certainty.[2] This thinking naturally leads to the deconstruction of absolute truth and absolute knowledge of God. Derrida and his contemporaries have convinced many people to make just such a rejection. His conclusion about "destructive discourses" has become the tunnel through which many have traveled to abandon moral absolutes and perpetuated our current cultural laziness concerning ethics.

However, N.T. Wright, a former bishop of Durham in the Church of England and a renowned scholar, argues we *can* know the center. We may not begin directly *at* the center, but as we look closely at the circle, use the right tools, and then critically and realistically work—admitting our errors and correcting them as we go—we will find our way to the exact middle. He calls this being a "critical realistic." We can know the object by looking at it, checking ourselves, looking at it again, and checking that our calculations follow principled laws. By being critical during the process of becoming more accurate, we can know truth.[3]

Many of us today are walking around with a melted-chocolate notion about truth and morals. We believe it isn't possible to have specific and defined statements. We think moral absolutes are historical myths and erroneous assumptions. We plead ignorance about the overarching scheme of things. This worldview is inaccurate. There are time-tested laws and statements that cannot be refuted. We must throw out the notion that truth doesn't matter.

TRUTH IS FLIGHT

Think of the principal of flight. It took years of theory and study before people began to understand how to create lift that could somewhat counteract the law of gravity. The special shape of an airplane wing (an airfoil) is designed so the air flowing over it will have to travel a greater distance, and faster. This results in a lower pressure area and produces lift. Lift is the force that opposes the force of gravity (or weight). It depends on five factors: (1) the shape of the airfoil, (2) the angle of attack, (3) the area of the surface exposed to the airstream, (4) the square of the air speed, and (5) the air density.

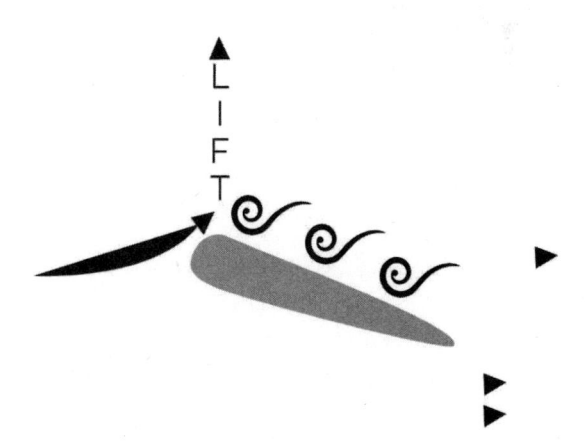

Every time we get into an aircraft, we bank our lives on this truth. We travel the entire surface of the earth believing these principals are true and putting our faith in them.

Why stop at the principle of flight? We know truths about many other things, and we should respond to them as well. We need to get rid of the lame it's-above-my-pay-grade excuse and those-were-my-grandma's-morals attitude. We can't just say, "That's an antiquated idea," and dismiss it just because it's inconvenient. We can't say "the modern person" is different.

William Gairdner says, "Ideology is destiny."[4] Those who thrive in companionship have clear guidelines for marriage. We might disagree. We certainly fight. We lament our bentness. However, we let truth correct us whenever our sinfulness gets in the way. We listen to wisdom and allow ourselves to be changed. Proverbs 8:1,11 says, "Does not wisdom call out? Does not understanding raise her voice?.... Choose my instruction instead of silver, knowledge rather than choice gold, for wisdom is more precious than rubies, and nothing you desire can compare with her."

People are building homes where our children have love, guidance, protection, a vision for life, and where both of their parents remain faithful to each other because they hold to specific commands that guide their living. When we get off course, these guidelines correct us and enable us to get back on track. It would be impossible for us to survive without them. But we had to throw out the culturally popular mantra that truth doesn't matter.

Three
SECURITY GATE B: TRUST CHRIST

FAITH IS VITAL

By now, I hope you have accepted the idea that you *can* know truth. I hope you have rejected agnosticism (which says "we can't know") because it is logically and experientially false. But where does truth come from?

This may be the most important question of human history. We Christians derive our answers from our deep convictions about God's existence and His kingship over the earth. We believe that God possesses ultimate power and sovereignty over the world. We also believe He has revealed Himself to us personally so we might live in peace with Him. When we rebel and darken our thinking through sin, God sends out messengers to explain the rules of His kingdom. In the past He spoke through prophets, but in these last days He sent His Son to be the way, the truth, and the life.

This is the story of what we call "the gospel." Jesus died as a substitute for each of us. Jesus, the Son, took our punishment so we could be called sons of God and be reconciled to Him. Because of this, God gives eternal life to anyone who turns to Him through faith in Jesus' death on the cross, burial in the tomb, and resurrection from the dead. Furthermore, God's gaze reaches right into our living rooms and bedrooms. We receive His mercy when we allow Him to speak into our current life situations and when we submit to His plan. If we obey Him, we experience blessings. If we deny Him, we experience condemnation.

At one point we all ask, "But how can we know these things? Where can we search for ourselves? How do we know these things stand over and above other beliefs?" We might not be convinced at the onset, or we might start with a different worldview. We might doubt God reveals Himself and His truth to us through creation, the Bible, and the incarnation of Jesus

Christ (which means "in-flesh" or "in-bodily form"). But each of these three disclosures is convincing and compelling.

WE SEE TRUTH IN CREATION

Humans are affected emotionally, psychologically, and physically by choosing either wisdom or foolishness. This is clearly observable. The more "bent" we become, the more destructive our lives become. One can quickly see the joy of living with wisdom over and against the curse of being foolish. Building on the beach offers a great view, but when a hurricane passes through the area, the home will be destroyed. Building with a solid rocky foundation is much wiser (see Matthew 7:24).

These variations in the human experience occur because God designed the world with His wisdom. He reveals Himself and His divinity through the laws of nature in the cosmos. We see the omniscience of the Designer when we look at the universe He created, from the wildflowers to Mars. We see the wisdom of the Creator when we live our lives according to His material laws. His wisdom is so interwoven into the fabric of our world that when we reject His plan, it tears at the fibers. If we were to sweep our hand across the building blocks of life, our folly would knock away order and create a backdraft of hazardous decay.

Proverbs 8:22–31 is a great poem of God's creation in which we see how God used wisdom to create the world. Wisdom is defined as "applied truth," and when the Lord created the world, He applied truth to bring about its order. If we want to create something beautiful, we must apply truth to bring it about.

> The LORD brought me forth as the first of his works,
> > before his deeds of old;
> I was appointed from eternity,
> > from the beginning, before the world began.
> When there were no oceans, I was given birth,
> > when there were no springs abounding with water;
> before the mountains were settled in place,
> > before the hills, I was given birth,

before he made the earth or its fields
> or any of the dust of the world.

I was there when he set the heavens in place,
> when he marked out the horizon on the face of the deep,

when he established the clouds above
> and fixed securely the fountains of the deep,

when he gave the sea its boundary
> so the waters would not overstep his command,

and when he marked out the foundations of the earth.
> Then I was the craftsman at his side.

I was filled with delight day after day,
> rejoicing always in his presence,

rejoicing in his whole world
> and delighting in mankind.

In this passage, the Bible lets the many abstract principals of wisdom speak as if they were in human form. In this living picture, wisdom is personified as a beautiful and important woman. She is a craftswoman God uses to build the whole world, and she calls out to the world to listen to her instruction. She calls for us to recognize God and live by His wisdom. This explains why there are physical ramifications for both obedience and disobedience, because God built the universe on the principals of wisdom. We can ignore them or we can apply them, but each decision will bear consequences.

The properties of matter and energy are God's handiwork, and the behavior of all organisms comes from His storehouse of knowledge. Our human ability for art, structural design, industry, and technology all come as we apply His understanding and act with His kind of disciplined behavior. In the same way, and more importantly, our effectiveness to love, to create thriving homes, and to establish just societies all rest on our conscious decision to cling to God's wisdom as evidenced in creation. If we desire to transcend the human corruption of this world and be victorious over our bentness, we must trust the infinite God who is exceedingly beyond us in knowledge and character.

I know these answers to life and relationship questions are different from most. I've been in many rooms where guys and girls get into conversations with me by laughing at these thoughts. "You're a very nice Christian," they say, mentally patting me on the head as they have another drink. Then they say out loud, "You're loco though; not in the real world. I like my own choices, thank you very much. Now leave me alone." But I really do believe truth must come from someone else in order for it to transcend human corruption. It must be true beyond our reality. It must be true from beyond human manipulation. It must come from distant shores. We have to reject the attitude that Jesus is outdated, because all the wisdom of creation and the pain of corruption tell us otherwise.

The beauty of a healthy newborn baby, the warmth of a smile, the embrace of a parent, the peaks of the mountains, the complexity of one cell—each of these remind us of God our creator. On the other hand, the ugliness of slavery, the coldness of a sneer, the exasperation of bitterness, and the rejection of divorce remind us of evil. We do not accept them as the counterparts of good. However, they do remind us of God's goodness, because we appeal to Him to redeem us from these things. Romans 1:20 reads, "Since the creation of the world, God's invisible qualities—his eternal power and divine nature—have been clearly seen, being understood from what has been made, so that men are without excuse."

The beginning of wisdom is to fear God (see Proverbs 1:8). In order to be wise, we must admit we don't create truth or morality, and we must acknowledge *the One who created it*. In the same way the laws of flight have always existed but were only recently discovered and used for human flight, the laws of morality have always existed, and we need only discover and utilize them for our relational life.

"SPIRITUALITY" DOESN'T COUNT

Everybody wants to be "spiritual" these days. But when we talk about faith, we are not talking about being spiritual. This is just a new term that has replaced "being religious." It has little meaning. It's the same old mantra, but in a different wrapping.

When I was a kid, adults used to say the same thing to my dad when he spoke about his faith: "I'm religious; I'm just not practicing." I always thought, *How do you not practice something you believe in?* It would not make sense if professionals acted that way. "I'm a doctor, but I don't read medical journals or understand anything about health. I am a mechanic, but I don't fix cars. I'm a farmer, but I don't plant seeds or harvest."

I was sitting on a plane a few months ago, traveling to Chicago from Toronto. It is a short flight, about an hour and a half, and I was a reading a Christian book. The young man sitting in the window seat beside me commented I must be a Christian because of the book I was reading. I responded that, yes, I was a Christian. Then I asked him, "What do you believe?" His response to me was typical—very open and friendly. "I am spiritual," he said. "I don't like formal religions, but I am taking some classes on how to be more spiritual."

After an hour of conversing and asking him some basic philosophical questions, it became obvious to me that my new friend could not give any shape to his spirituality at all. In essence, he didn't believe anything. He just called anything that felt chocolate-chip-ooey-gooey "spiritual." At that point, I asked if I could reflect back to him three things I had observed within his thoughts to see if I was hearing him correctly.

He granted me that permission, so I continued. "Number one," I stated, "you probably believe in a greater higher being. Is this correct?"

"Yes," he responded, "that it is correct."

"Second," I continued, "in your desire to be more spiritual, you are hoping to connect with that divine force or supreme being, because you feel the need to lean on something greater than yourself."

"Yes," he said, "I would love to connect."

"Third," I said, "you don't like to be told what to do."

He chuckled. "Yeah," he responded, "that's exactly why I don't like formal religions, because they don't allow me to think or act the way that I want to."

Isn't this the story for most of us? We believe in God, or many gods, or a supreme power. We want to know Him, to know what is right and wrong, and to have boundaries. Furthermore, we hope to understand what He is doing and the greater purpose of life. But at the same time, we don't like to be told what to do. We reject systems that tell us what to do and exchange them for a kind of nothingness. We use age-old expressions like, "that's outdated," "that view is antiquated," or "that's good for you, but not for me," when we just want to do what we want. But if this is our story, we need to see the writing on the wall.

This expression means a dramatic event is near, so we need to be attentive. For example, we might say, "The writing is on the wall for them—they're about to break up." Or, "The writing is on the wall for him—he's cheating and is about to get caught." Did you know the expression actually comes from the Bible?

There is a story in the book of Daniel in which God literally writes a message of judgment on a wall in the palace of the Assyrian king Belshazzar. God writes a pronouncement of judgment that reads, "You have been weighed on the scales and found wanting" (Daniel 5:27). Daniel, a slave exiled to that land, interprets the writing, and Belshazzar dies the same night. Can you image God revealing a message to someone and it coming true almost immediately? In this situation, Belshazzar was using stolen items from the Temple of God in Jerusalem to praise his gods of gold, iron, bronze, and silver. God told him his pagan spirituality and personal ambitions as king were not good. His behavior was not right.

Now, can you imagine some modern actions that would be displeasing to God? For example, a man leaving his family just so he can have sex with an attractive young woman? Or a woman choosing to bring another man into the home when her husband is out working? Many of us can imagine these things, because many of us have experienced some form of this parental foolishness as children. As the dust settles and everyone points fingers of blame, we know they just want us to give our blessing to the new situation.

However, as we weigh the options, we can see the situation for what it is: flat-out destructive. It was created out of dysfunction, and now it turns into pain. It doesn't solve anything. We had hoped our parents would remain faithful to each other—that they would be gentle, kind, patient, faithful, and affectionate to one another. We know our homes should have stayed unified. We have weighed this new arrangement and found it wanting.

People let pride, impatience, sexual immorality, idol worship, and falsehood ruin their relationships every day. They fail to manage their behavior because they do what they think is right in their own eyes. They do what they want out of bitter envy and selfish ambition and hurt their loved ones because of their aimless living and shapeless morals. They slide into malicious habits, and these habits destroy lives. These things *should not be*, and we need to see them for what they are. They are not the ideal. They do not have to be our future reality. We all know there is a higher standard.

With this in mind, we need to know "the word of God is living and active. Sharper than any double-edged sword, it penetrates even to dividing soul and spirit, joints and marrow; it judges the thoughts and attitudes of the heart. Nothing in all creation is hidden from God's sight. Everything is uncovered and laid bare before the eyes of him to whom we must give account" (Hebrews 4:12–13).

We see the higher bar and understand how to move toward it through the teachings of the Bible. We recognize God reveals Himself specifically in Scripture—that He has given us His Word so we can know what to do and are not found wanting. As 2 Timothy 3:16 states, "All Scripture is God-breathed and is useful for teaching, rebuking, correcting and training in righteousness, so that the man of God may be thoroughly equipped for every good work."

ONE PART *FIRE*, ONE PART *ICE*

In the book of Revelation, Jesus spoke to the church of Laodicea about the shapeless way they were living. He said, "I know your deeds, that you are neither cold nor hot. I wish you were either one or the other! So, because you are lukewarm—neither hot nor cold—I am about to spit you out of my mouth" (Revelation 3:15-16).

In our culture, "to be hot" means to be excited about something, while "to be cold" means to be opposed to it. However, Jesus is drawing His analogy from drinking-water. Hot water is soothing, warming, and stimulating; cold water is refreshing, cooling, and shocking; but lukewarm water is not good at all.

Think of it this way. If you go to a hot springs resort, you go to relax in its warm comfort. If you boil water, you kill germs and drink it confidently. Hot water is extremely useful. At the other end of thermometer, if you go swimming in a cold river, you become refreshed. If you drink cold water, you are energized. Cold water is useful too. But what is the middle temperature like? Well, if you swim in a lukewarm or stagnate pond, you will deal with mosquitos, leeches, and algae. You will smell. And you dare not drink the same tepid water, because it is infested with bacteria. The conditions will make you sick. Lukewarm water is good for nothing, just as lukewarm spirituality is good for nothing. We must avoid it.

Many of us live without faith because we accept only the kinds of teachings that please us and validate our current actions. In reality, we do this because we don't like to be told what to do. We use the excuse that we can't really know anything so we will have the freedom to do what we want. But this is not a logical and defensible argument. We are just making things up as we go along to get people off our backs and avoid stinging questions. We like doing what we want, and we haven't stopped to think if it's wise or true.

It is unwise for us to live without the hot-debating-kind-of-passion for truth—the kind that makes us call for justice and argue for virtue. It is also foolish for us to journey through life without the cold-stiffening-kind-of-passion for truth—the kind that slows foolish momentum until we calculate and weigh the results. We need to have some fire in our bellies or ice in our minds to prepare is for our future.

In the book of Revelation, Jesus goes on to teach about the *source* of truth. He says, "You say, 'I am rich; I have acquired wealth and do not need a thing.' But you do not realize that you are wretched, pitiful, poor, blind and naked. I counsel you to buy *from me* gold refined in the fire, so you can become rich; and white clothes to wear, so you can cover your shameful nakedness; and medication to put on your eyes, so you can see" (Revelation 3:17-18).

Here the wise Teacher depicts the shapeless life for us. He describes it as a naked and blind person trying to convince everyone else he is well dressed. This is a person who lives like the emperor with no clothes. The man is delusional. He has been swindled. He has misunderstood the frailty of his own situation. He is confident, but woefully unprepared. He is "wretched, pitiful, poor, blind and naked."

Are you the college student or young professional who likes to be "religious" but hates anything that "censors" your life? Maybe you grew up in the church, and now you reject all the rules. Maybe you're living for the bar scene and holding nothing back because you want connection or freedom. Maybe you're taking up yoga to bring you closer to inner peace. Maybe you enjoy talking about different philosophies, but you resist the exclusive claims of Jesus—that He is the only way to God. These shapeless and formless attitudes will sabotage you from having a safe journey. If you choose to fly without foundational beliefs, you will veer off course and crash the plane.

In Jesus' analogy in Revelation 3, the "gold" he counsels us to buy from Him symbolizes wisdom, and the "white clothes" symbolize purity. He is telling us to come to Him to be made wise and pure. Wisdom comes as we give shape to our lives through obedience to His good words, and purity comes through the forgiveness we find through belief in Christ's death and resurrection. We can't be ambivalent, dirty, and arrogant on our own but must believe in Christ and be forgiven from our sins so we can live to the fullest. This is what Jesus offers us, for God's wisdom and forgiveness are found in Him. He said, "I am the way, the truth, and the life. No one comes to the Father except through me" (John 14:6).

The security guards at the gates are there to prevent dangerous things from entering the planes. They stop people from bringing hazards onto the aircraft that could cause destruction. In the same way, God encourages us to throw out our excuses and find truth before we self-destruct. Truth is the foundation on which everything rests—including relationships. It defines what is good behavior and what is unacceptable. It gives meaning and direction to our actions. It helps slow us down or fire us up. It tells us there is reason to have self-control.

Furthermore, Jesus is the source of truth. He is the Word of God in real skin. He came down from God to be our teacher, shepherd, and example. He said, "If you hold to my teaching, you are really my disciples. Then you will know the truth, and the truth will set you free" (John 8:31-32). He validated the Old Testament with miracles and taught His disciples with authority. Therefore, we can trust Him.

FOLLOW CHRIST

The Christian *is* different. And sometimes it's hard to be different because others look at us funny. It can be lonely following Christ. It is a struggle to swim against the main current of the stream. It is hard to stand on the slip'n slide when everyone else is riding by, grabbing onto your ankles with laughs and giggles to drag you down with them.

Sometimes, being a Christian is extremely hard, because we do want to be just like everyone else. Our old self wants the bigger house, the faster car, and the hot mistress. It is often hard to fight our own corruption. I am an enemy to myself—a Jekyll and Hyde. You can point your finger at me and see all my blemishes. You can recite my imperfections, smell my rottenness, and catch me in my lies. It is hard for me to walk on a narrow path, because my old sinful self wants to straddle the broad one. One foot in good; one foot in evil. It is a battle. Yet Jesus calls out to us and empowers us to become clean through *His* power.

Jesus commanded us to have different and higher standards, and He provided a way for us to seek out those standards. First, He taught us His wisdom, which underpins the building blocks of life. Second, He performed miracles to prove His divinity. Third, He died on the cross to pay the punishment of my sin. Fourth, God raised Him from the dead, because it was impossible for death to keep its hold on Him. Finally, He gave us the Holy Spirit, who reminds us about what He taught. Through faith, His wisdom, and in His sacrifice, we have tasted and experienced that He is good. The life of a Christ-follower is satisfying, because it rests completely on Jesus Himself.

Tree63, a fantastic South African band, once wrote this lyric: "Your blood speaks a better word than all the empty claims I've heard upon this earth." I believe this with all my heart. Jesus came and died so I might live. Most of His first disciples died so His lessons might be passed on. In the shed blood of Christ, God's wrath is appeased. God remains just, but also justifies those who ask for forgiveness through Jesus. At the same time, He gives us selfless, invested, triumphant love, which exceeds the empty, bent, and fleeting claims of men.

That's it, my friends. I want to follow Christ because Christ's commands have never failed me. There is only Jesus. He is the source of truth; He defines love. I am always more enriched when I follow Jesus because He leads me to love (both its source and applications). Even though it is a battle, which I often lose, when I actively pursue Christ's standards to put sin behind me, I see a more pleasant and peaceful way through turmoil.

Will you trust Jesus? Will you follow in His footsteps? Where others have exchanged God's commands toward virtue for things that are dark and futile, will you cling to these promises and commands so your life will be full of virtue? Will you leave the darkness behind and walk toward the light?

ACCEPT NEW IDEAS TO HAVE NEW LIFE

If you aren't a Christian yet, you can put your faith in Christ today. Here are some scriptures that explain what it means to trust God, believe in Jesus Christ, and have your sins forgiven.

> I am the LORD your God, who brought you out of Egypt, out of the land of slavery.
>
> You shall have no other gods before me.
>
> You shall not make for yourself an idol in the form of anything in heaven above or on the earth beneath or in the waters below. You shall not bow down to them or worship them; for I, the LORD your God, am a jealous God, punishing the children for the sin of the fathers to the third and fourth generation of those who hate me, but showing love to a thousand generations of those who love me and keep my commandments.
>
> You shall not misuse the name of the LORD your God, for the LORD will not hold anyone guiltless who misuses his name.
>
> Remember the Sabbath day by keeping it holy. Six days you shall labor and do all your work, but the seventh day is a Sabbath to the LORD your God. On it you shall not do any work, neither you, nor your son or daughter, nor your manservant or maidservant, nor your animals, nor the alien within your gates. For in six days the LORD made the heavens and the earth, the sea, and all that is in them, but he rested on the seventh day. Therefore the

Lord blessed the Sabbath day and made it holy.

Honor your father and your mother, so that you may live long in the land the Lord your God is giving you.

You shall not murder.

You shall not commit adultery.

You shall not steal.

You shall not give false testimony against your neighbor.

You shall not covet your neighbor's house. You shall not covet your neighbor's wife, or his manservant or maidservant, his ox or donkey, or anything that belongs to your neighbor (Exodus 20:2–17).

These commands are from God's Word. They explain His standards for living. Notice the first four concern our requirement to love God. He doesn't take idolatry lightly. He doesn't want us to worship anyone or anything else. The latter six concern our love for our neighbor. God set these instructions in place so we would live in accordance with His goodness among other people. He gave us these commands to strengthen our relationships and societies. However, as I've mentioned before, we are bent and need to be rescued from our constant rebellion against God and His commands.

There is no one right before God, not even one (Romans 3:10).

For all have sinned and fall short of the purity of God (Romans 3:23).

So I find this law at work: When I want to do good, evil is right there with me. For in my inner being I delight in God's law; but I see another power at work in the members of my body, waging war against the law of my mind and making me a prisoner of the power of sin at work within my members. What a wretched man I am! Who will rescue me from this body of death? (Romans 7:24-24).

Paul teaches there is a battle going on within us. Left to our own abilities, we would fail. However, there is good news: God has created a way to forgive us. He loves the world so much that He sent His Son into it to die for us. Whoever believes in Him will live and have eternal life.

If you confess with your mouth, "Jesus is Lord," and believe in your heart that God raised Him from the dead, you will be saved. For it is with your heart that you believe and are justified, and it is with your mouth that you confess and are saved. As the Scripture says, "Anyone who trusts in him will never be put to shame" (Romans 10:9-11).

I will continue to build my case on Christ and the Bible. If this is too much for you to accept right now, don't turn away. I do hope you will accept it all—that even today you will believe in your heart, confess with your mouth, and be saved. But if you can't do that, keep reading. Think critically. Test these claims. You can find Christ, the truth, if you look for Him.

ACCEPT OLD IDEAS TO FIND NEW DIRECTION

If you are like many Christians today, you may have more cultural data in your mind than you do biblical data. It seems the church has an ability to over-spiritualize feelings and under-scrutinize truth claims. We tend to lose our first love of Christ and settle for things that reflect the world (see Revelation 2).

Maybe you've traded the power of truth for the cultural lies of shapelessness. Maybe you've been distracted from living out the commands of Jesus. Maybe your parents struggled to be different from the world and never taught you about practical Christian living. I encourage you to study your Bible. Learn to appreciate key passages like Exodus 20 and Matthew 5–7. Journey through the Proverbs and mark the ones that apply to you. Read and reread 1 Corinthians 6:12-20 and Ephesians 6:10-18 until they are impressed on you. Then live them.

When you are challenged with temptation, overcome it by learning from God's Word and praying through the temptation. Stop and think of what's good, change your course if needed, and rededicate yourself to God's wisdom and purity.

Finally, be strong in the Lord and in his mighty power. Put on the full armor of God, so that you can take your stand against the devil's schemes. For our struggle is not against flesh and blood, but against the rulers, against the authorities, against the powers of this dark world and against the spiritual forces of evil in the heavenly realms. Therefore put on the full armor of God, so that when the day of evil comes, you may be able to stand your ground, and after you have done everything, to stand. Stand firm then, with the belt of truth buckled around your waist, with the breastplate of righteousness in place, and with your feet fitted with the readiness that comes from the gospel of peace. In addition to all this, take up the shield of faith, with which you can extinguish all the flaming arrows of the evil one. Take the helmet of salvation and the sword of the Spirit, which is the word of God. And pray in the Spirit on all occasions with all kinds of prayers and requests. With this in mind, be alert and always keep on praying for all the Lord's people (Ephesians 6:10–18).

ACCEPT GOOD IDEAS TO PASS ON GOODNESS

If you are like many parents today, you may be failing to remember what God has done for you in your generation. Since the sexual revolution, many Christian parents have just gone along with the world's ideas of romance. In reality, the world's ideas of love are tantamount to the sands of the desert. God has allowed many in our generation to taste the emptiness of this kind of living so they may realize they can only depend on His Word to find direction. In some sense, we live the same desert experience as Israel did when they wandered aimlessly.

> Remember how the LORD your God led you all the way in the desert these forty years, to humble you and to test you in order to know what was in your heart, whether or not you would keep his commands. He humbled you, causing you to hunger and then feeding you with manna, which neither you nor your fathers had

known, to teach you that man does not live on bread alone but on every word that comes from the mouth of the LORD.... When you have eaten and are satisfied, praise the LORD your God for the good land he has given you. Be careful that you do not forget the LORD your God, failing to observe his commands (Deuteronomy 8:2–3,10–11).

When we fail to remember the lessons God has taught us, we don't impress His commands on our children. We let them do what their peers want. When this happens, a generation grows up without knowing the Lord, and they inevitably do "what is evil in the eyes of the LORD" (Judges 2:10).

Do you "love the LORD your God with all your heart and with all your soul and with all your strength" (Deuteronomy 6:5)? As you believe and obey the Lord, you direct your love for Him toward Him with great adoration and affection. After this, you can direct your love for God toward your neighbors, your family, and even your enemies. This is sincere love of the heart, not in word only. Lips represent what's going on outside, while the heart represents what's going on inside. It is our inward being, our seat of decision, which is equivalent to the rational part of our humanity. Matthew Henry describes it as "inwardly, and in truth, solacing ourselves in him."[1]

The immaterial and eternal part of us is our soul—our will, our determination, and our eternal trajectory. Our moral and rational heart should never be separated from our eternal hope. Rather, the things we love through our heart should be so deeply pure and ingrained in us that we will love them eternally in the presence of God. We must externalize this eternal love, this willed love, with all our strength. We must love the Lord with our muscles. People have often said, "Actions speak louder than words." James puts it, "Faith without deeds is dead" (James 2:26). It is by our physical parts that we follow God's moral commands.

Are you helping your children through meaningful actions? Everything starts from inside and flows out. So hear God. Believe in God. Love God. Obey God. As Jesus said to His disciples:

No good tree bears bad fruit, nor does a bad tree bear good fruit. Each tree is recognized by its own fruit. People do not pick figs from thornbushes, or grapes from briers. The good man brings good things out of the good stored up in his heart, and the evil man brings evil things out of the evil stored up in his heart. For out of the overflow of his heart his mouth speaks (Luke 6:43–45).

As evidence that you love God with all your heart, you need to impress God's commands on your children. You need to "talk about them when you sit at home and when you walk along the road, when you lie down and when you get up" (Deuteronomy 6:7). As Reverend George Rawlinson said, "Truth and godliness is to be perpetuated by means of home training."[2] Matthew Henry also noted, "Means are here prescribed for the maintaining and keeping up of religion in our hearts and houses, that it might not wither and go to decay."[3]

Personal meditation on Scripture, passion for prayer, and ownership for ministry will result in the life-on-life Christian formation of our children. Through discipleship, their hearts will grow stronger, their minds will grow clearer, and their words will be bolder. It is like the process by which radio waves emit from a tower to take their message of hope out to the surrounding area. As the signal strengthens, it covers new ground.

So imprint God's love and His commands onto your children. Some call this "walk-along, talk-along, bring-along discipleship" Others have expressed these actions as, "I do, we do, you do." But it starts with you!

Four

SECURITY GATE C: WHY FRIENDS BECOME LOVERS

OUR NEED FOR SIGNIFICANCE AND SECURITY

Remember, when I use the term "friend," I mean people who are more than acquaintances. I am not speaking about people with whom you are friendly, like classmates, teammates, club members, or family connections. You will live life with members of the opposite sex and enjoy times with them in public. You will have men and women who laugh with you, and you will go out for dinner with them in groups. These are often called friends and, in a broad sense, they are your friends.

However, when I speak about friendship, I specifically mean someone with whom you spend time one-on-one in order to build a greater connection. You might spend time with this person because you have the same interests, because you are attracted to his or her personality, because you can talk to that person easily, or because you feel lonely. As you've grown somewhat connected to the person in public, you now spend more time with him or her in private in order to strengthen the bond of mutual affection.

Affection is a feeling of fondness. You genuinely enjoy a person and feel positive feelings when he or she enters the room. If given the choice, you would spend time with this individual beyond the group. This kind of person might identify with your past, share experiences with you in the present (such as schooling, church community, hobbies, or interests), and might resonate with your vision for your future.

In this kind of friendship, I firmly believe that men and women can't just be friends without feeling the pull toward sexual intimacy. This pull creates new dimensions and adds physical stimulation to the relationship. When men and women bond emotionally, they also grow in physical attraction toward one another. You've already heard this. Now we will discuss why it occurs as a result of our basic needs.

I came across the work of Dr. Larry Crabb, a marriage counselor and author, while Sarah and I were training to go overseas. We were learning why we should stay in our own marriage and encourage others in polygamous cultures to be monogamous. During those lectures, I came to realize why friendship attraction exists and why male and female relationships are so important to us. Dr. Crabb writes, "Being a person centrally involves an identity which requires security and significance to function effectively."[1]

This statement tells us we each exist with two basic needs. First, we need to be significant to someone. We need to feel sufficiently worthy of attention or noteworthy in someone else's eyes. Second, we need to be secure. We need to feel safe, stable, and free from fear or anxiety. We need to feel fixed so as not to give way, become loose, or be lost. Let's take a look at each of these specific needs.

OUR NEED FOR SIGNIFICANCE

We adopted our second daughter, Galilee-Ling, from China, and I am scared at times. Our first daughter, Maylah, brims with confidence because she grew in Sarah's womb and has felt our love since the moment she entered the world. Galilee-Ling, however, grew in Sarah's heart first and had to endure three years apart from us.

I've seen how adopted children can feel insignificant because of the rejection they've felt from their birth parents. Our relationship with our parents is important to our sense of significance, because we find vast amounts of significance from their love and nurture. Sarah and I try our best to give our little girl all the love and nurture possible, because we want her to grow up knowing how immensely wonderful and valuable she is to us. She is awesome, but we will have to teach her about God's love and how she can find significance by trusting Him. We will also have to show her that she is loved and valued by pouring out affection and attention on her.

We will have to sacrifice our time to be with her. We will have to give up our treasures so she will be taken care of. We will have to direct our talents toward building her up. Hopefully, these actions will lead her to find much significance in our home.

Now, even though our relationship with our parents gives us significance and helps us understand that God has created us with value, we each move beyond the confines of our childhood home and begin to look for significance in other human beings. We will look for other ways to be significant in the world. If our parents have done a good job, we will carry a measure of confidence with us into this next stage. If our parents have struggled, this new environment will be difficult for us to navigate because we will not understand appropriate ways to find significance.

OUR NEED FOR SECURITY

A second basic need we each have is for security. This means we draw a sense of safety from our ongoing relationships. We don't just want to be significant to someone for short spurts of time; we want relationships that remain constant. Commitment and faithfulness provide us with security, which is why we experience so much grief when we lose a loved one. That person's constant love gave us security, and now we feel loss and vulnerability. The more permanent the relationship was, the more loss and vulnerability we feel.

For this reason, a long-lasting marriage provides one of the most powerful, unique, and special opportunities for a person to help another individual feel more secure. Two people who are committed to caring for one another for their entire lives have a rare opportunity to bring each other a greater level of security because they keep the feelings of significance constant. This type of security is not common. It is not found in common places. It is not found everywhere. It is only found in committed relationships. It is found in the home, consecrated by marriage, and cemented by faithfulness to one another.

In chapter 1, we looked at an article by Tracy Clark-Flory called "In Defense of Casual Sex." As we discussed, she provides a perfect example of the "hookup" attitude so prominent in our culture. However, even though it's clear this young woman doesn't completely understand her own experiences, she does understand how we each need permanence to give us security. She writes, "*The New York Times* recently ran a Modern Love essay by Marguerite Fields, a college junior, about her search for a boy willing to commit. Like me, she has worked her way through a number of men and says, 'I think what I have been seeking in some form from all of these men is permanence.'" Permanence is just another word for faithfulness. Feelings of security grow as we continue to be faithful to one another. We need this desperately.

Think of it in terms of a secret agent who has been betrayed by the CIA. He's always looking over his shoulder. He struggles with attachment and doesn't know whom to trust. The same happens with us. The more we expose ourselves to broken, short-term relationships, the more we anticipate betrayal and the harder it becomes for us to attach, trust, and remain objective. Or think of it in terms of a passenger going on a plane after 9/11. It is harder for that person to relax, trust, and enjoy the flight, because he or she fears there might be a terrorist on board.

GOD MADE US MALE AND FEMALE

In our quest to fulfill these needs of significance and security, friendship attraction begins to take place because God made us male and female.

My working definition of "friendship attraction" is that when men and women bond emotionally, they also grow in physical attraction toward one another. Friendship attraction generally occurs when women seek out relationships that emphasize friendship and men seek out relationships that emphasize sexual experiences. Women desire to be noteworthy in someone else's eyes by connecting emotionally with that person, and these relational experiences and verbal interests make them feel recognized. On the other hand, men receive recognition physically. They become interested in relationships in order to fulfill physical desires. Sexual experiences and physical activity make them feel fulfilled.

Harriet Wehner Hanlon, PhD, and her associates at Virginia Tech University examined the brain activity of more than 500 children aged two months to more than sixteen years. They noted one important difference between young men and women: "[While] talking is central to the friendships of females at every age...boys don't spend a lot of time talking to each other."[2] Furthermore, "when girls or women are under stress, they'll often look to each other for support and comfort. Not males. When boys and men are under stress, they usually want to do something physical."[3]

Even in situations where this is flip-flopped—where a woman finds more significance in sex or a man finds more significance in friendship—those individuals generally look for the opposite trait when seeking someone with whom to have a relationship. You've heard the expression "opposites attract." Thus, even the exception of the rule proves the rule of friendship attraction.

Friendship attraction occurs because men and women long to feel significant, but they find significance in very different ways. We are not the same. While there are exceptions and even perversions of this rule, we generally fulfill our needs for significance in uniquely male and uniquely female ways. Genesis 1:27 reads, "So God created man in his own image, in the image of God he created him; male and female he created them."

Have you ladies ever questioned why men want sex so much? Have you ever wondered why they rush into it and continuously obsess over it? On the other hand, have you men ever questioned why women want to spend so much time with you? Have you wondered why they desire to be out with you? The answer lies in significance. We find it differently. When our Creator made the genders unique, he made them *unique*. We are biologically different. We are rationally different. We were given different roles and bear different experiences. When we find significance, we find it differently.

> FRIENDSHIP: *a state of mutual trust and ongoing support; a person with whom one has a bond of mutual affection.*

> FRIENDSHIP ATTRACTION: *When men and women bond emotionally, they also grow in physical attraction toward one another because they generally fulfill their needs for significance in uniquely male and uniquely female ways.*

GOD DESIGNED SEX
TO JOIN HUSBAND AND WIFE TOGETHER

Many young men and women today have bought into the idea of "no strings attached" and are hooking up sexually. On the radio, I just heard a song with the lyric, "Do you want to make love or just fool around?" As if there is a difference.

It's difficult for me to say this in a way that you can really see it, so let me draw it for you. Diagram time! Okay, think carefully about the phrase, "No strings attached." What do you see? I see two unconnected shapes. If I sketch it, it looks like two horizontal lines on a page:

_____

_____

That's it. There is nothing binding them together. They are just railroad tracks journeying for hundreds of miles without any intersections. Now take the act of sex. As purely as you can, what do you see? I see two connected objects that are attached. If I sketch it, it looks like two lines intersecting at a specific point:

X

The lines are inter-coursing and cross each other. They are indistinguishable from one another. In the same way, sex connects people. It is physically impossible to deny this, and it's ludicrous to even try. In fact, we wouldn't like it so much if we *could* deny this. I am sure all of us realize this, but so much of the world operates is if it weren't true. The suggestion that someone can have sex without making a significant connection to the other person is a falsehood. As God said in Genesis 2:24, "For this reason a man shall leave his father and his mother, and be joined to his wife; and they shall become one flesh."

God knows it is not good for us to be alone. So he made the male gender to be strong leaders, lovers, and workers, and then made the female gender to be enduring partners, nurturers, and helpmates (see Genesis 2:18). The sexes each bring something to the table that compliments the other. They are not the same, but they do share a connection. They become attracted to one another because they naturally want to become "one" with the other part that fits with them.

Now, we are not insufficient alone. A spouse does not fill a deficiency, but a spouse does add strength to us. Women become attracted to the "otherness" of men, and men become attracted to the "otherness" of women. Women are drawn to the strength, valor, and character of the man. Men are attracted to the beauty, gentleness, and nurturing capabilities of the woman. This is why it is hard for women and men to remain just friends. We each have a natural inclination to oneness.

In Genesis 2:24, we see that this natural drive toward one another is satisfied in marriage, when a man leaves his home and makes a new one with his wife. Marriage enables two people to compliment one another. It beautifies the bride and makes the groom magnificent. Marriage binds the two to each another. Sex is the tool that then completes the binding process by joining the two together as one: "They will become one flesh." Two individuals who have sex become physically and emotionally connected in a unique way. They are not meant to be torn apart after that moment, because sex has welded them together.

Did you know that when you join with a woman in the bedroom you are binding yourself to her emotionally forever? Did you know that you are performing an act that is intrinsic to the nature of marriage? Did you know that you will never be able to make a clean break from that person? It's like taking two pieces of paper and binding them together with super glue. Just try to separate them. Or take a pitcher of blue sand and another of pink sand, and pour them into the same vase. Then try to remove one color so you are left with the original colors. It's impossible to do these things.

Once you've had sex with someone, you've joined with that person and will take pieces of him or her everywhere you go. This is why it's harmful to bind yourself to many different partners through sex, because you remain bound to each one. You must create sexual distance and moral boundaries to protect your future love, because sex makes you one with someone. You cannot have sex without "strings" attached.

Barbara Wilson, author and former director of sexual health education for the APRC in Sacramento, writes, "Scientists have discovered that during sex the brain releases a hormone called oxytocin to create a strong bond between people. This invisible bond works as a super-glue, permanently attaching us emotionally to a lover. This bonding happens with everyone with whom we have sex. Produced by the body's pituitary gland, oxytocin is not only released into the blood during labor, delivery, and breast-feeding in women; it is also released in men and women during sexual arousal and release."[4]

The presence of oxytocin helps us trust and relax. As it is released into our bodies, we feel bound to the one with whom we are joining. I've seen this with my wife and with every woman I know who has had children. There is a deep and instant bond between mother and child during delivery and breastfeeding. As a mother, Sarah felt obligation and dedication to our children immediately after birth. As a father, I bonded with my kids slowly as we built relationships with each other over time. I didn't feel truly connected to my kids until they smiled at me, or said something to me, or actually asked for me. When they related to me, I felt my love and devotion for them surge. It was not this way for Sarah. She bonded instantly with our children because of oxytocin.

Most new moms share this experience unless something is out of order. They release oxytocin during labor and breastfeeding, which binds them to the child. The presence of this hormone brings them instant unity. If you try to separate a young mom from her infant, you will hurt her deeply, because she has already bonded with her child hormonally.

Think of the implications of this. If both sexes release this same hormone in the midst of making love, it makes perfect sense they would also feel bonded together from that moment. This is why we must keep ourselves pure. We can't just sexualize ourselves aimlessly, because if we do we will be bonded chemically to many different partners. In 1 Corinthians 6:18, Paul says, "Flee sexual immorality. Every other sin that a man commits is outside the body, but the immoral man sins against his own body." God created us to enjoy sex, but He created sex to bond us together with one other person.

The biological discoveries about the sexes and sexual release explains how we are bonded together instantly during sex. However, I hope in this chapter you have also learned *why* we are bonded together: God *designed* sex to join husband and wife together for life so they can minister to each other. As they share sexual and emotional experiences and fulfill their commitments to one another, it increases their feelings of significance and security.

Men and women were meant to compliment each other. It's good for a man to find a woman who will help him be a better man. It's good for a woman to find a man who will help her be a better woman. But we need to wait to bind ourselves with that person until we have joined together in marriage. For in marriage—through having children and creating a home—we find great power as our home becomes a collaboration, a mosaic if you will, of many lives converging and colliding with synergy and harmony.

In Malachi 2:15-16 we read, "Has not the Lord made them one? In flesh and spirit they are his. And why one? Because he was seeking godly offspring. So be on your guard, and do not be unfaithful to the wife of your youth." Sex is about becoming one. Marriage is more than just two individuals falling in love. The family unit is a foundational institution for church and society. God designed the marriage of a man and woman with a grand vision in mind.

TO THE GENTS ABOUT THE LADIES

Guys, I don't think you will find a woman who says she doesn't care about security and significance. For the most part, women are aware of their internal need for these things. Women enjoy being cherished. They love to be thought of and cared for. They love it when men make small talk and play games. They love being adventurous in relationships. Women want to be safe and free from anxiety. They want to be part of something meaningful.

As you can probably guess, women don't find significance through sex. They are far more satisfied when a close friend makes them feel valued through companionship. Friendship is where a woman finds trust, fun, and compatibility. As a male friend shows interest and listens to her, she thrives on their mutual understanding and acceptance. She finds common joy in sharing experiences. She encounters a safe place where she can let her hair and her guard down. She bonds as she shares similar experiences and interests with this companion.

For a man, companionship is the ultimate form of sacrifice by which he fulfills his decision to love a woman. He embodies that devotion through time and shared experiences. A wife finds great comfort when he drives a stake into the ground and says, "I will not leave your side." This protects her from jealous feelings, makes her feel wanted and significant, and enables her to fulfill her deeper desires to have a family and nurture children. She needs more than a one-night stand to feel this way. She needs to be fixed beside him as a companion. She needs to feel he sets her apart above all other women. She clings to him emotionally for this assurance and support.

An Example from the Bible

The book of Ruth tells the story of two star-crossed lovers, Ruth and Boaz, whom God used to demonstrate courageous, down-to-earth, and compassionate dedication. When Ruth's first husband died, she courageously moved with her mother-in-law to a foreign land in order to care for her. Ruth sought to provide for their basic needs and went to pick wheat in a neighbor's field. Like most immigrants, she had to work hard to survive in the new land. It was there that Boaz saw her need. He was faithful enough to take care of her, and then, eventually, he married her. Through this story, we can see how much women value faithful companionship:

> Then Boaz said to Ruth, "Listen carefully.... Do not go to glean in another field; furthermore, do not go on from this one, but stay here with my employed maids. Let your eyes be on the field which they reap, and go after them. Indeed, I have commanded the servants not to restrain you. When you are thirsty, go to the water jars and drink from what the servants draw."
>
> Then she fell on her face, bowing to the ground and said to him, "Why have I found favor in your sight that you should take notice of me, since I am a foreigner?... May I continue to find favor in your eyes. You have given me comfort and have spoken kindly...."

Boaz took Ruth, and she became his wife, and he went to her. And the Lord enabled her to conceive, and she gave birth to a son. Then the older women said, "Blessed is the Lord who has not left you without a redeemer today, and may his name become famous in Israel" (Ruth 2:8–10,13; 4:13–14).

The key words in this passage are "take notice of," "comfort," and "redeem." Boaz took notice of Ruth. He joined into her life. Then he acted to bring comfort to her by being generous. Finally, he redeemed her from her widowed state by becoming her husband. Notice how the older women saw the value in Boaz—they said, "May he become famous."

GETTING THE EQUATION IN THE RIGHT ORDER

It is important for women to find a male friend who is enjoyable to be with and ready to be faithful. The first part brings her significance, while the second part makes her feel secure. Sex has little to do with this part of the equation, for her sexual responsiveness is a byproduct of her feeling significant and secure. Women don't want sex to *find* significance or security; they enjoy sex when they *have* significance and security. It is a pleasure, but not an imperative.

WOMEN
FRIENDSHIP = SIGNIFICANCE
+
FAITHFULNESS = SECURITY
SEXUAL RESPONSIVENESS

Men, did you get that? *A woman wants to marry a best friend who will engage with her emotionally and demonstrate commitment to her.* Read that sentence again and again! Memorize it! It's a woman's expectation and hope for her future marriage. It's natural and good. While she will enjoy sex, it won't be the way she will feel most accepted by you—and she generally won't need it as often as you do. This is why she will want to move slowly. She will enjoy your friendship, but she won't feel as motivated to give herself to the joys and pleasures of sex until you have solidified your friendship into faithful commitment. If she were to do so, she would be betraying herself.

In her book *Kiss Me Again*, Barbara Wilson writes, "When a man and a woman become friends first and save sex for marriage, sex enhances the [emotional] intimacy that's already been established. But many of us have reversed the order. We became lovers first, without developing a friendship. When the newness subsides, we discover that we need more than sex to feel close. We need to be good friends."[5]

Why Is This the Case?

The reason this works the way it does is because God has given women a great vision of home. He has built into women the understanding that a nuclear family is the safest place to have children and develop harmonious love. Now, I know that sounds ancient and not at all modern. In fact it is, because God said it: "She watches over the affairs of her household and does not eat the bread of idleness. Her children arise and call her blessed; her husband also, and he praises her: 'Many women do noble things, but you surpass them all'" (Proverbs 31:27–29).

God declares it is noble for women to have a mind for their home. Even if women in our culture are driven to go after careers, money, independence, power, and fame, God still invites them to partner with men in order to build homes. As a result, most women have an internal drive to be a wife and a mother over and above these other things.

Men, we should be celebrating these noble attributes of the women who call us to companionship in order to build healthy homes. By having sex, women enjoy intimacy, minister to their husbands' needs, and bear children. They are drawn into relationships through the hope of home and family. They settle down and make home out of the thought of friendship and family. We should be their best supporters in this.

A Story About True Longing

Listen to what Solomon's bride says of him on their wedding day as she anticipates the sexual intimacy of their wedding night:

> My beloved is mine and I am his;
> > he browses among the lilies.
> Until the day breaks
> > and the shadows flee,
> turn, my beloved,
> > and be like a gazelle
> or like a young stag
> > on the rugged hills.
> All night long on my bed
> > I looked for the one my heart loves;
> > I looked for him but did not find him.
> I will get up now and go about the city,
> > through its streets and squares;
> I will search for the one my heart loves.
> > So I looked for him but did not find him.
> The watchmen found me
> > as they made their rounds in the city.
> > [I asked,] "Have you seen the one my heart loves?"
> Scarcely had I passed them
> > when I found the one my heart loves.
> I held him and would not let him go
> > till I had brought him to my mother's house.
> Daughters of Jerusalem, I charge you
> > by the gazelles and by the does of the field:
> Do not arouse or awaken love
> > until it so desires....
> Who is this coming up from the desert

> like a column of smoke....
> Come out, you daughters of Zion,
> > and look at King Solomon wearing the crown,
> the crown with which his mother crowned him
> > on the day of his wedding,
> the day his heart rejoiced... (Song of Solomon 2:16–3:6,11,10).

Notice how, even though the entire passage is sexual in tone, sex doesn't represent her true longings. First, she says, "My beloved is mine and I am his." Second, she says, "Who is this coming? It is Solomon on the day of his wedding." These are direct comments about the security and significance she finds in the relational connection with her spouse. They are one, which makes her feel great. They are committed, which makes her feel confident.

She goes on to say he "browses among the lilies," and she encourages him to "be like a young stag on the rugged hills." The white lilies symbolize her vagina, which is pure and not defiled by other partners. The rugged hills refer to her breasts. So, this is an invitation for her husband to join with her in a love dance. She welcomes his sexual aggressiveness; in fact, she is being sexually aggressive here by inviting him to play on her body. She calls him to enjoy the pleasures of sex. She, herself, is "faint with love" (Song 2:5; 5:8). But it only comes after she reflects on their oneness—her with him in the context of their enduring unity. She is excited for sex because it is their wedding day!

The bride goes on to describe her continual longing to be with her husband. She imagines that after they have made love, he goes out at night—possibly to do kingly business or keep watch over the city during a time of threat. In this daydream, she puts her safety at risk to find him, because she can't wait for him to come home. She searches in dark places and meets the guards of the city. She is anxious, because he may not come back. What if he loses interest in her? What if he has gone to another woman? What if he dies during a violent conflict? She looks for her husband and holds tightly to him when she finds him.

This is a story about her need to have his commitment. She fears he won't come home to her at night. She fears she won't have him close by and won't be able to hold on to him after being intimate. Will he choose her or his job as the king? Will he choose her or his battle-forged friendships with the warriors? Will he choose her or find a mistress? Will he come with her to her mother's humble house instead of the royal palace? Will they be together and hold fast to each other? These are her questions. Throughout the song she goes on and on about her desire for him to come home, to ignore the other girls, to limit his employment responsibilities, and to journey with her. She is longing for his body, but she is also longing for his permanent presence. She will let him have his fun, and she will enjoy that great wine-tasting time too, but she wants him to be with her.

Listen to how she warns other women: "Daughters of Jerusalem, I charge you by the gazelles and by the does of the field: Do not arouse or awaken love until it so desires." This refrain occurs twice in the song. Both times, the beloved wife has just imagined making love to her husband. Both times, she refers to the gazelles and does of the field. She is connecting the image of these other two other female groups who bear offspring in the spring to the love-making of her wedding day, which is also in the springtime. She does this to command young women, who may have the sensual longing for sex because of their own fertility, to wait until marriage.

This proverbial warning is the wise, godly, woman pleading for all women to keep free from sex until their wedding day. They should wait until they have love—*committed-marriage love*—with the kind of man who will come home to them every night. The wise woman knows sexual love should be postponed until the person who is willing to say "I do" arrives.

The wise woman says to the girls, "Search for love, but do not connect with a man until he has shown himself awaked to be responsible, full of character, and committed to you. Long for a male friend's physical and emotional presence, but do not awaken yourself sexually until he commits to be faithful to you by marrying you. Do not have sex until you commit to each other and are bound together permanently."

Men, This Is Important Now and in the Future

Do you see how this all fits together? Before marriage, you have to be self-controlled and committed to purity in your dealings with women. You must work hard at the friendship and hold back your sexual advances. Understand this now, and gain real wisdom about life. Stop being deluded by television and movies.

Never pressure a young woman to be sexual. It goes against what she really needs from you. If you truly want to fulfill a woman, if you truly love her, demonstrate love and faithfulness first. Women will be most satisfied by your friendship and your companionship. You will have to show her your willingness to come home happily every night in order for her to be truly fulfilled. Friendship will make her feel significant, and faithfulness will make her feel secure. After these are in place, she will have received from you what she needs and deserves. Then, the greatest sex in the world develops from an exclusive, long-lasting, loving marriage.

This is important for your future. Many men miss this. You need to stop focusing on yourself in this area and demonstrate marriage commitment and friendship *before you have sex*. Your wife will be overjoyed with your purity. She will also greatly appreciate your thoughtfulness and foresight, and ultimately it will bring her what she longs for.

TO THE LADIES ABOUT THE GENTS

Women, the men who tell you they don't long for significance and security are just plain ignorant. Men all want to be affirmed, respected, and accepted. They also need stability. Rejection hurts them and discourages them. They thrive when they have a female counterpart who supports them, cheerleads for them, and is faithful to them. No doubt, men want security and significance for sure.

However, as I've already mentioned, men don't find the same level of significance in friendships as women do. Men find significance in the continual combination of friendship and sex. Friendship is the area in which a man is encouraged and supported. As a female friend helps and supports him, he finds meaning as he responds to her needs, is thoughtful of her uniqueness, takes care of her, and comes to know her better than anyone else. This makes him feel significant, and he finds companionship and camaraderie in the friendship. However, relational experiences will not fulfill him completely. Sex is an important ingredient to foster significance. For guys, words only say so much. The physical connection completes the picture.

This happens because sex is a dramatic and passionate act of vulnerability for a woman, by which she accepts and literally connects to her friend. He feels comforted during this time, which makes him feel worthy in a unique way. Sex itself is physical communication; it is a physical way to say, "I love you." When it is reserved for him alone in a marriage, it makes him feel she wants him around in a unique and special way. He needs more than just a long conversation to feel this accepted. He needs to be fixed to her body, feel desired by her, and to physically cling to her to fulfill this need.

An Example from the Bible

In the Bible, the prophet Isaiah portrays the city of Jerusalem as a woman who will provide comfort to her people out of her abundance. Just as a woman nurses her child or physically consoles her husband with her breasts, Jerusalem would give people refuge and supply in the future. While Isaiah is primarily saying something about the city by drawing an example from the everyday life of a wife, he is also saying something in general about women.

A woman often brings comfort to her children and her husband through her body. A woman's physical body is important to the heartbeat of the home. "Rejoice with Jerusalem and be glad for her, all you who love her; rejoice greatly with her.... For you will nurse and be satisfied at her comforting breasts; you will drink deeply and delight in her overflowing abundance" (Isaiah 66:10-11).

This helps to explain why sex is so meaningful for men. As this passage shows, the woman through her body offers him satisfaction, comfort, and delight. She has many other characteristics to bring to the relationship, but a man finds great satisfaction, comfort, and delight in her body. This type of communication is irreplaceable. It is vitally important for him to find a spouse who is both enjoyable as a friend and sexual as a lover. The first element brings him a certain level of significance, and the second completes the picture.

Getting the Equation in the Right Order

This means a man struggles in friendships where sexual intimacy is not an active factor in the equation. He will want sex in order to feel more significant in a friendship. When sex and friendship are both active parts, his loyalty is ignited and he gains deeper significance from the relationship. As a wife remains faithful to these elements, it helps him feel secure. Friendship and sex are both "first order."

MEN
FRIENDSHIP
+
SEXUAL INTIMACY
=
SIGNIFICANCE
+
FAITHFULNESS
= SECURITY

Ladies, did you get that? That is the sentence you paid for. *A man wants to marry a best friend and sexual partner who will be faithful to him.* Men will always pursue sex if you offer them friendship. It's their expectation, because they hope for those two things in marriage. It's natural. It's good. They really don't just want sex, but they also don't just want friendship. This is why men will hang out with you and then quickly rush to touch you. He enjoys your friendship but longs for the satisfaction, comfort, and delight of your body. Humorist and author Mark Gungor explains, "The way to a man's heart is not through his stomach. That's six inches too high."[6]

Dr. Douglas Rosenau, professor of human sexuality at PSI, suggests in his book *A Celebration of Sex* that men want sex more often because they use lovemaking as a primary way to connect with their mates. Their sexual desire can seem greater because the sexual part of the relationship carries a great deal of intimate meaning for them.[7] Men want friendship because it adds meaning to their lives, but they want sex because it makes them feel uniquely and intimately significant. It carries greater meaning for them than it does for women.

Why Is This the Case?

The reason this works the way it does is because a man's intense sexual drive comes from the presence of testosterone in his body. Testosterone creates a fairly consistent desire for sex in males. However, while this explains *how* men desire sex as often as they do, biology alone fails to explain *why* they were designed this way. It excludes men's feelings and ignores the meaning they find in sex. It also excludes an explanation of God's design for men.

Men are not just sex-machines running around trying to adjust to a daily chemical imbalance. Rather, God created them to be drawn to women through sexual attraction and friendship in order to call them into leadership and service for the home. Sex is so meaningful to men that they try to secure its frequency by staying in a committed relationship. Sex calls them home.

This is God's design for drawing men into loving, lasting marriages. Without this design, men might not see the necessity to be a loving father or a caring husband. With it, however, they are ready to conquer the world, save the girl, protect their children, and provide for the home. They settle down and establish homes when they see the possibility to make love and live in friendship.

A Story About True Longing

King Solomon of Israel once wrote this in a love song to his wife:

> You have stolen my heart, my sister, my bride;
> > you have stolen my heart
> with one glance of your eyes,
> > with one jewel of your necklace.
> How delightful is your love, my sister, my bride!
> > How much more pleasing is your love than wine,
> and the fragrance of your perfume
> > more than any spice!
> Your lips drop sweetness as the honeycomb, my bride;

milk and honey are under your tongue....
Your stature is like a palm tree,
and your breasts are like its fruit.
I said, "I will climb the palm tree,
I will take hold of its fruit" (Song of Solomon 4:9–11; 7:7–8).

Notice how Solomon finds so much significance in her body. The Bible gives us insight into the male's perspective, and it gives us permission to share in this perspective as long as we are engaged in marital relationships. Men are attracted to women physically and emotionally. In this biblical book about love, a paradigm for marital love, the husband focuses greatly on her body and some on her friendship. He is driven by two priorities: sex, and then friendship. Together they bring him great satisfaction. God designed men to want these kinds of intimacies. These are the two components that draw men into relationships.

He first calls her his "sister." By this he is not saying she is his literal sister, but is just making a comment on their closeness and their common calling to rule over the kingdom. The *Bible Sense Lexicon* refers to the relationship as a close female friend for whom there is affection as for a sister.[8] John Wesley states, "[She is] the greatness of his love, which cannot sufficiently be expressed by any one relation."[9] He knows her as well as he knows one of his own family members. They talk. They walk. They laugh. They fight—all that family stuff. He knows what frustrates her. He knows who frustrates her. He understands her pains and insecurities. He understands her deep inner strength. He also knows her as a queen as she shares in his burden to attend to the affairs of the state. One commentator writes, "[She is] a sisterly sharer of his royal rank and name. She is queen, as he is king."[10]

I remember when people used to say that Sarah and I acted more like a brother and sister than boyfriend and girlfriend. I used to think, *Sarah is going to me wife; don't be gross.* But then I came to understand what they meant. They were observing that we were very close to each other, which was true. After just a short time of courting, I knew Sarah better than I knew my own sisters. I knew her better than her family did, and she knew me the same way.

Sarah is strong and resilient. She is tough and has a stiff upper lip when she wants to hide her emotions. She can hold it together. Yet she is also sensitive to God's leading. She has a deep desire to be obedient to God and resolve conflict, which makes her vulnerable. She has a desire to communicate and solve problems. I came to know this quickly.

I also came to know her as a woman who passionately cares for others. I felt called to be a pastor, and she was comfortable being a pastor's wife. So, she now shares the burden of my ministry within the church. She carries the responsibility with me of telling others about Jesus. She is a sister in ministry. She's my "sister" and my bride. I love her for this, and I often reflect on the strength and support she provides. Today we still laugh and cry together. We go for walks and play board games like Settlers of Catan. We read our Bibles together and try to learn what God is saying to us as parents. We value our close companionship.

Solomon goes on to say, "How delightful is your love." Here is the transition: he *is* interested in her body. He's staring at her eyes. He's staring at her breasts. He is thinking about making love. He's expecting their time together will be better than the very best wine. He is intoxicated by the thoughts of kissing her. Milk and honey are under her tongue. He can taste her. He is completely infatuated with her sensuality.

Throughout the song, Solomon goes on and on about her beauty and her body. This doesn't mean she was a perfectly shaped woman or that she was only an object to him. It means he saw her as a perfect lovemaking partner. He longed for physical contact with her and thought about that moment. As long has he had their friendship and sexual unity, he felt significant. He was happy. If the relationship stayed that way, he wouldn't ever be worried about it. Sex and friendship help a man feel significant in a relationship.

It really is that simple. Sex cuts tension for men. Sex brings them release. Sex creates within them a greater aptitude to open up emotionally and relationally.

Ladies, This Is Important Now and in the Future

Don't close your eyes to this simple truth, because it is important. You have to wise up and be vigilant with your own purity. You cannot be deceived into thinking that men just want to be friends. You cannot let them sway you into giving them your body. This burden is on you, because you are responsible for yourself. I have already addressed the men. Now you must take responsibility for your actions, because if you compromise in this area, you will produce massive insecurity in yourself.

You need to accept this to protect yourself. You need security, and yet security only comes with commitment and permanence. Men will always find significance in sex. They are more sexual than you and will never just want to be friends. In fact, a good friendship will only spur deeper desires for sex within them. It will coax along those natural desires. For this reason, if you spend lots of time with a young man but have no intention of becoming intimate with him, it will often frustrate him. He will feel hurt and rejected without you being aware. On the other hand, if you become sexual with a young man, end up detached from him, and then repeat that cycle five or six times, you will be haunted by insecurity. You will have baggage, because God designed you to be fulfilled in oneness.

Hold the boys off until they mature, have a sense of responsibility, and have established character. Hold them off until they have the ability to commit to marriage. Your friendship and sexual intimacy will bring pleasure to any young man, but he will not offer security to you in return unless you wait for the right time. You want to wait for a man who demonstrates virtue and temperance.

MIND THE GAP

There is a sign in the London Underground that reads, "Mind the Gap." I read it during my first journey through London Heathrow's new terminal 5. It encourages people to be aware of the space between the train and platform. It is the same with men and women. There is a difference between the sexes in relation to significance and security, and we need to be mindful of that fact. Ignoring the gap leads to injury.

Hebrews 13:4 says, "Marriage is to be held in honor among all, and the marriage bed is to be undefiled; for God will judge those who have sex outside of marriage and those who have sex with someone other than their spouse." This is what often happens to girls. A young, foolish, and selfish man wants to jump into bed with a female friend because he's looking for significance. He already finds a level of this in their friendship, but now he is looking for more. He feels that he is not yet significant enough to her because she hasn't fully accepted him.

The young woman, with a great heart and hopeful intentions, gives in to him before any real commitment is established. The guy finds his sense of significance when she accepts his sexual proposal, but he leaves because he isn't mindful of her feelings. So the young woman is left hurt and incomplete, because she didn't retain her friendship, even though she gave herself physically. She will anticipate betrayal from the next man.

This is what often happens to guys. Young women can think androgynously about relationships—that boys also only want friendships. So one young man with a good heart and proper intentions works hard at a friendship with a girl, with the intention it will grow into an intimate relationship. But the young woman has no clue about this—she is just having fun while the guy pines away. She might even think other guys are "hot." He's trying to make the friendship perfect enough for the girl to cross into intimacy, and he might even be ready for marriage and serious about commitment. But that doesn't happen, because the woman is oblivious to the connection between friendship and sex for him. When he tells her his feelings, she says, "Let's just be friends." He is left feeling hurt and rejected, because she is happy with "just friends."

In many such friendships, the men end up feeling rejected because they longed for the relationship to grow into intimate acceptance. They don't feel significant when the friendship remains non-intimate. These same friendships leave women feeling pressured, disillusioned, and frustrated, because their male friends push them to be their girlfriends with all the physical intimacy that comes with it. On the other hand, sex outside a committed friendship will lead to hopeless dirtiness. If it doesn't leave that feeling immediately, the memories of casual sex will stay with the individuals into future relationships, and they will bring hurt and frustration into those places. This is plain, simple, and true.

You can't ignore these driving forces. You must mind the gap and keep meaningful distance between yourself and the opposite sex. You must create limitations on your friendships with the opposite sex in order to keep pure and avoid immature rejection. You must only pursue an intimate friendship with a person of the opposite sex when you are ready to transform that friendship into a marriage.

We will talk about the specifics later. Just go with me for now.

Five
BOARDING AND DEPARTURE

AUTHORITY FIGURES IN OUR LIVES

Just as you rid yourself of wrong notions at the security checks, the boarding and departure process ensures you are equipped with proper knowledge. There is a shift, for the objectives of the two areas are entirely different. The security gates protect the plane from dangerous sabotage, while boarding and departure process ensures passengers have the proper documentation and safety information. One stops harmful things; the other promotes positive things. So, at this point, I want to make sure you have the right information to move forward.

Proverbs 12:1 says, "Whoever loves discipline loves knowledge, but he who hates correction is stupid." People who have legitimate authority over us have the right to give orders, make decisions, and enforce obedience. We don't naturally like authority figures when they try to correct us, but each of us have legitimate authority figures with roles like parents, grandparents, uncles, aunts, church elders, community leaders, teachers, and employers. If we learn to recognize and honor legitimate authority figures, we will learn how to be teachable and seek guidance rather than willingly being held hostage to our own bentness.

On the other hand, there are people who would say, "Let us eat and drink, for tomorrow we die" (1 Corinthians 15:32). They will influence us to be short sighted and shrug off legitimate authority. Paul responds, "Do not be misled: 'Bad company corrupts good character'" (verse 33). A source of corrupt pressure comes from those who have no right or experience to guide us. If we learn to recognize and reject this illegitimate authority, we will learn how to be free from pressure and oppression.

Here are the three things we need—three things that act as passport, boarding pass, and on-ground instructions. First, God gave us *parents*; therefore, we are to obey our father and mother. Second, if we accept Christ, God gives us a *Christian family*; therefore, we can learn from the experiences of that church family. Third, God gives us the gift of *friendships*; therefore, we should choose them wisely.

These ideas are old, yet they have become unfamiliar. Hear me out about them. Maybe you are laughing right now. Maybe your parents are distant and distracted. Maybe you have never attended church and don't plan to do so. Maybe you enjoy the party lifestyle and are loyal to the friends who join with you in it. Bear with me. It will make sense after some explanation.

These ideas are rooted in history, because most historical cultures were called strong-group cultures. In these settings, individuals sought what was best for the group, not for themselves. They were willing to put their personal satisfaction at a lower priority in order to promote group health. Western society used to be built on church-group culture, or Christian culture, and hold to its values and virtues. This shaped the Western world from the fourth century until now. Western free economy was built on the assumption that the family unit was the training ground for its future citizens and a place of production. The family, not the public/state school, prepared the student for life. For these reasons, the family (a close group) and the church (a larger community group) played a greater role in the life of a young adult. This is old stuff.

Yet these ideas have recently become unfamiliar because of a transition toward individual autonomy (self-law). A number of generations have now grown up being told, in general, to reject parental and church authority to pursue their own pleasures and peer desires. We are now a called a "weak-group culture." or at least a peer-group culture. To a large degree, individuals no longer take into account the needs or advice of the family group but only pursue their own interests.[1]

We listen to peers who share our opinions rather than parents who try to direct them. We don't ask broader questions like how our personal actions will better the lives of our immediate and extended family, or what we can sacrifice to promote another sibling's wellbeing, or what we can do to help out in the long term. We don't say to ourselves, *If I date that guy, sleep with him, and then break up, how will that affect my parents now and my children in the future? If I go after that girl, knowing how much conflict surrounds her, how will that affect my parents now and my children in the future?* People just don't raise these questions as often as they used to raise them.

In fact, these are so foreign that you might be asking yourself, *How could my future children even be affected? How could my parents be affected?* Here is a brief list:

- Teen pregnancy affects children, parents, and any future mate.
- Sexually transmitted diseases affect children, parents, and any future mate.
- Emotional scarring affects all close relationships.
- Divorces that occur as a result of promiscuity affect children and parents. Like begets like, and our attitude shapes the next generation.

COMMON REASONS FOR IGNORING PARENTS AND THE CHURCH

It's impossible here to elaborate on the global reasons why these cultural shifts have occurred, but it would be prudent to name some of the most significant reasons why you might want to ignore parents and the church. Some of the reasons are scary and scarring.

First, *your parents might be brutal.* They might be domineering, exhausting, and controlling. They might be weak, exhausted, and out of control themselves. Many adults have failed marriages, and many struggle to understand God's authority themselves. They have an entire list of "family commands" or "family values" that don't make sense and don't help you navigate tight corners.[2] Even though they live with hopes to be positive examples for you, they may not have much to offer you in the area of wisdom and maturity.

I know what it's like to fail my kids. I hope to be patient and gentle, but I often teach them impatience and harshness by my example. Because of this, one of our unwritten family commands is to be indirect or sarcastic, which I must change over time by changing my example. Preparing them for marriage is an area I don't want to fail them. I want be involved. I want to be helpful. This will require further work on my part to grow. However, I've had many conversations with young men and women whose parents are distant during this important time. Their dating advice is limited to "whatever makes you happy." These parents struggle to talk about character, preparedness for marriage, or Christian maturity, and they don't ask questions to find out about sexuality. There is often the normal, "We love you and want you to be happy," but many parents have shallow advice and lack of wisdom. I am sure that I, too, will struggle in this area when my children become young adults and push my limitations. So I understand why you may not trust your parents with their limitations.

Second, *you might have never darkened the doors of a Bible-believing church.* Maybe your parents didn't value church attendance, so they never took you. Maybe media and the pervasive secular humanism in culture made you skeptical. Or you had a hurtful church experience and never went back. Either way, it's made it difficult for you to even imagine a church family should play a major role in your choice of a spouse.

If you've never attended church, or if you've had a bad experience, the local church can be a strange place. I understand why you might be skeptical. Even if a local church is healthy, being a part of a church family isn't easy. It's a place where you are taught, cared for, and held accountable. There are conditions placed on your life. It takes time and sacrifice. You have to sit and listen and be willing to take correction. This is not easy. If a local church is unhealthy, terrible harm can occur: priests molest children, pastors lead money scams, and parishioners live unreconciled lives. This makes it almost impossible to trust some churches.

Third, *you might have bought into our culture's lies.* Our society is obsessed with license, the freedom to behave as one wishes, even if those ways result in excessive or unacceptable behavior. Our culture has become fixated on doing everything sensual and explicit. We want restrictive laws thrown away, and we want to redefine the common ideas of appropriateness. Purity, modesty, and caution have become the three ugly sisters to lust, outrage, and vanity. Virtue, competence, and prudence have become the three boring brothers to rebellion, outrage, and self-absorption.

For these reasons, many people don't accept the authority of the family or the church. For them, the family and church have moved away from the center of the city. They have been placed on the outskirts, where they can't be heard in the chaos of downtown.

However, despite these frustrations with parents, and despite the ongoing tensions that occur when sinful people gather together into a local church community, and despite our culture's obsession with license, God gives young people three specific commands. The first and most important one is this: *Obey your parents and listen to their advice* (see Exodus 20:5; Proverbs 1:9). The second is *guard your life and beliefs closely as the older generation teaches you self-control* (see 1 Timothy 4:15; Titus 3). The third is *choose your friends wisely* (see Proverbs 1:15; 1 Corinthians 15:33).

YOUR PASSPORT: OBEY AND LISTEN TO YOUR PARENTS

God gave you parents so you would learn how to respect His authority and gain wisdom. You are at the stage of life where you need to be mature, but this is not a magical journey, nor should you try it alone. Orphans have a hard time figuring out life precisely because they have been left abandoned and left without instruction. At this point in your journey, it is key for you to listen to your parent's advice. Good parental advice is a valuable possession.

Did you know that airlines consider individuals to be minors until they are seventeen? You have to make special arrangements to fly without your parents if you're under seventeen. Now, if the adult flying age is seventeen—when you can just walk through a building, sit on a plane, and get picked up afterward—what should the mating age be? Seriously. Just because you can physically have sex and date, it doesn't mean you have the emotional maturity, experiential capacity, or the provisional opportunity to act like an adult. What I mean is that you're unprepared to go it alone!

Don't take this too harshly. Many of you are wonderful, bright, and full of potential. But also don't take it too lightly, for it has truth in it. You are not wise in years, you haven't developed fully, you don't have experience in many regards, and you don't support yourself by your own two hands.

Some of you young world travelers might be recalling the times when you traveled alone, but I assure you that *your parents* made arrangements for you.

Do you get my drift? The airport doesn't want to deal with children who haven't learned to respect their rules or understand their precautions. They depend on parents to take that responsibility. They don't want be liable for someone who is acting like a child without parental supervision. I can't imagine my seven-year-old flying alone. If he had the confidence to try to fly alone, he certainly wouldn't know how to go about it. He'd get lost at the first pub for food and football. If you found him stranded, you'd first try to find his parents. If we weren't nearby, you'd direct him to an adult in a position of authority. You wouldn't direct him to kids his own age or to a gang. You'd find an adult—parents, if possible—who could really help.

In fact, you can measure young peoples' maturity by their obedience to their parents. Proverbs 17:2 says, "A wise servant will rule over a disgraceful son, and will share the inheritance as one of the brothers." If a father sees his son or daughter disregarding instruction and acting disgracefully, he will give even the employees of his company more credit and attention than his children.

Dating is no exception. Too many young adults are goofing around behind their parents' backs. Too many students are lying about their physical behavior in relationships. Too many individuals are not letting their parents guide and disciple them because they translate correction as condemnation. Too many young girls are being pressured and bullied without protection. Too many boys are on the loose without restraint. Parents have no idea what is really happening between the sheets, in the car, at a friend's house, on the couch, or walking home from school, because their children are flat out hiding it from them.

Honoring Your Father and Mother

God gave us ten commands in the Bible to create boundaries and define the moral law. They tell us where the outer boundaries lie. They are walls to the halls. They define the direction. They are the soup bowl. Did you know only one of those commands was given with a promise? It is the fifth commandment, which says, "Honor your father and your mother, so that you may live long in the land the LORD your God is giving you" (Exodus 20:12).

At this time in Israelite history, the Jewish people were about to invade Canaan. The people in that land lived different lives from what God wanted for his people. The Canaanites lived out many sexual perversions and even sacrificed their children to idols. God gave this fifth commandment so godly parents would pass on godly principles to godly young people. The only way to not dilute the solution or corrode the foundation with the acid of the foolish nations was for the young men and women to listen to their parents as they taught them God's standards and wise proverbs.

God put your parents here to protect you, not to oppress you. If you do not submit to their wise counsel, the Bible says you are foolish. "Son do not stray from instructions of your father, do not leave the teachings of your mother. They will be like a gold chain around your neck.... A wise son heeds his father's instruction, but a mocker does not listen to rebuke.... A fool spurns his father's discipline, but whoever heeds correction shows prudence" (Proverbs 1:8–9; 13:1; 15:5).

Your parents are here to lead you. Their authority over you does not end when you are fourteen, fifteen, or sixteen. In Canada, you are not considered an adult until the age of eighteen, when you can vote. An even better measurement for independence is maturity, which means there is no magic number excusing you from their care. If you are mature in your ability to function with wisdom, then parental authority disengages. However, if you begin your pursuit of happiness by betraying the main authority figures in your life, you will be undone. The ropes of the sail will come loose too soon, when you can't hold them tightly yourself.

Have you ever noticed the difference between a ball of string that has been spun with precision and hard work and one that had just been crumbled together in an entangled mess? Like a fishing reel, life is complex. Life requires management and necessitates organization. If you ignore good teachings from your parents, you will find yourself more like the ball wrapped up in knots—good for nothing, ready to be thrown out, and frustrating all other things. Your job as a young person is to learn how to submit to your parents so you will learn how to choose good.

So, when your parents give you boundaries about being alone with another person, or give you instructions about being home at a certain time, or restrict you from going to certain places, or intervene in a relationship where you are moving too fast, or are trying to protect you from yourself and your immaturity—listen to them!

This is what God puts on you. You are responsible for listening and obeying. Even with their limitations, you will be blessed by obeying your parents.

An Equation for Maturity

In my own life, my father gave me an equation to help me become a man under his guidance. This is my elaboration of his basic ideas:

- Increased character/self-control = increased trust
- Increased trust = increased responsibility
- Increased responsibility = increased competency
- Increased competency = increased freedom
- Increased freedom = Moving my butt out of the house so I could get married, enjoy companionship, survive in the working world, and have lots of sex.

Let me break this down for you, peel back the layers, and show you the individual parts by themselves. These categories were helpful for me as a young man, and I see them unfolding with our oldest son, Simon. We are right at the beginning of the journey to adulthood with him. After a night with his friends, something happened to make him feel that he needed to make some changes. He said, "Dad, how do I become mature? How do I get people to take me seriously?" I responded, "It starts with self-control so that you build trust."

Increased Character/Self-control = Increased Trust

When my daughter Maylah, who is six now, makes up her mind to disobey me, it can be flat-out dangerous. There have been times when we've been on busy streets and she's made up her mind to go her own way to keep up with the boys. During those times, when we are walking in the midst of traffic, if she pulls her hand from mine to stop or run ahead, I snatch her up into my arms so she doesn't get hurt. I know that children her age lack logic and self-control, so I don't trust her to be able to do too much on her own.

If you are fourteen to eighteen right now, it is possible for you to be logical and self-controlled. If you want to be treated like an adult, you must learn self-control. You must transition from being the child your parents do not trust to the young adult your parents do trust. You need show them you're not about to run into traffic or make dangerous decisions because you lack judgment.

Increased Trust = Increased Responsibility

If you learn self-control, your parents' trust in you will translate into giving you increased responsibility. For those of you who are younger, this might include staying at home while they go away for the evening, or being able to drive the car, or being allowed to go out of town on your own. For those of you in college, it might include managing the family business for a few weeks in summer, or moving out of your parents' home. At any age, these responsibilities should also include getting income-generating jobs, finding mentoring relationships, and managing a budget. As you prove yourself trustworthy, you will be given more responsibility.

When I was sixteen, my father rebuked me after I had broken his trust. I had been caught for shoplifting. "Grow up," he said. "Your grandfather fought in a war when he was your age." I had to learn this lesson by having my responsibilities stripped away because I had lost my father's trust, but that statement changed my life. It shook me awake from the idea that I was expected to forever be a child pursuing fun. Even though the effects weren't instant, it was a turning point. My grandfather had been trustworthy enough by the time he was a teenager to be responsible to fight for our country's freedom. I got a vision of what that meant. I realized I could do so much more with my life, and I didn't need to wait until I was old. If I gained my father's trust back and maintained the responsibilities I had, then

I too could be trusted to do something demanding with my life.

So, if you're twenty-one and still living on your parents' dime, with no responsibilities for your own sustainability, you've got to change something now! It's clear that you are not being very trustworthy.

Increased Responsibility = Increased Competency

The reason why you have to be both trustworthy and responsible becomes clear as you seek to make successful choices. As you successfully take on more responsibility, you learn to operate independently. At first you practice under your parent's supervision, and this maturation forms into competency. Then, when you have demonstrated your ability to achieve, the umbilical is severed. Competency is the ability to succeed at a task or project.

One of my niece's female friends is an amazing wakeboarder. She does backflips and tail grabs and all of it. I remember being on the boat with her one time when she tried time and time again to nail the backflip. Her father sat on the back of the boat encouraging her, checking to see if she was warm enough, and making sure she was strong enough to keep trying (we were getting late into the evening). He was there to suggest different ideas and give feedback.

She was exhausted and water-logged, but her basic technical skill, combined with her ongoing determination to listen to advice, along with her bravery and practice, allowed her to finally complete the move. After landing it a number of times in a row, she was finally competent enough to do it consistently. Now it is natural and easy to her. It is second nature.

This is what I want for you: for successful living to be natural and relatively easy. Life will always be challenging and difficult, but you can react with experience and insight to make it better. Proverbs 14:23 reads, "All hard work brings a profit, but mere talk leads only to poverty."

Increased Competency = Increased Freedom

Your ability to be competent will be matched by your parents' willingness to give you greater freedom. The more you do life successfully with competency, the more freedom you will get. Proverbs 22:29 reads, "Do you see a man skilled in his work? He will serve before kings."

As you become skilled, you will get freedom to say, "This is what I choose." If your parents are confident that your choice will be successful, or at least reflect appropriate values and standards, they will be much more willing to say, "It *is* your choice. Go for it." Once you have the ability to act on your own without making immoral or immature decisions, you will be ready to enjoy increased freedom from your parents. Eventually, it will turn into the milestone moment where you are ready to move out.

It Is a Journey of Valleys and Mountains

There is no magic age for all this to happen, and the formula doesn't always flow in one direction, but thoughtful parents will be involved in the process. They won't always get it right with you. You won't make the transition to adulthood without failing them at times. However, the end goal will be for you to become your own individual who chooses wisdom on your own, rather than staying dependent on them because you aren't trustworthy or competent.

Whether you pursue education, a career, singleness, or marriage, you should aim to be competent when you arrive into young adulthood. Parents and students are setting the age of accountability and responsibility far too late in life. This does not mean parents should stop supporting their children, but you must let their nudges and tugs do the work to move you toward maturity.

YOUR BOARDING PASS: GUARD YOUR RELATIONSHIP WITH GOD

God gave you parents to train you and teach you discipline. But what about your parents' limitations? What if you find yourself saying, *My parents fall really short in their advice, their wisdom, and their vision to help me become an adult?* What if your family commands are anger, selfishness, and emotional hostage taking? What if they do not speak to each another or manipulate each other for selfish desires? What if they just leave you to grow up by yourself, or exasperate you with misguided and ungodly expectations?

On the other hand, what if your parents are great but don't have the experience to help you in certain areas? I could never teach my daughter to do backflips on a wakeboard—I would need someone to help her who has done it before. This is a problem for all of us at times. The best parents I know expose their kids to trustworthy adults.

For this reason, God has provided the church. He has given you the opportunity to find a church family through faith in Jesus and the determination to allow others to help your immediate family. You can learn through their wisdom in areas where you and your family fall short. As it has been said many times, "It takes a village to raise a child."

Good parents are active with their children. They love them. They teach them. They apprentice them. They get them involved in the greater life of the church. They love them. But they also welcome other voices. They trust other adults and peers to speak into their young peoples' lives. These parents have life-on-life relationships with their kids. They are not hands off and letting "professionals" do the work. They let their children foster beneficial life-on-life relationships with other adults and peers. In Ephesians 4:11—15, Paul says:

> So Christ himself gave some to be apostles, prophets, evangelists, pastors and teachers, to equip his people for works of service, so that the body of Christ may be built up until we all reach unity in the faith and in the knowledge of the Son of God and become mature, attaining to the whole measure of the fullness of Christ. Then we will no longer be infants, tossed back and forth by the waves, and blown here and there by every wind of teaching and by the cunning and craftiness of people in their deceitful scheming. Instead, speaking the truth in love, we will grow to become, in every respect, the mature body of him who is the head, that is, Christ.

There are some powerful truths in this text. First, *the leaders of the church are to build up the people for works of service.* These works include parenting, loving a spouse, worshiping God, learning to trust God, learning how to work, treating neighbors with love, sharing the story of Jesus, and so forth. The church builds people up. When someone is deficient in one area, the church is available to help that person become efficient.

Jesus himself thought it was wise and powerful to establish the church to train people, so he commanded pastors to lead men and women to be holy and helpful. This helps individuals undo any "family commands" or "family attitudes" that have contradicted pure living. It helps to undo the character and personality flaws that each of us have. It also helps us overcome our incompetency.

Pastors and mature church family members can help your parents where they fall short. They can correct them, instruct them, and even rebuke them when needed. They can instill in them faith, hope, and love. They can come alongside and spur your parents on toward love and good deeds. They can feed them with God's Word and teach them how to study it. And pastors and church family members can be there for you too! They can train you in the areas you need. They can include the young with the old to help you gain competency and self-control and give you insights beyond your years.

A second truth found in Ephesians 4:11—15 is that *we all become fully mature through the greater understanding of Jesus.* The leaders of the church, who are mature in Christ, pass on this understanding to the next generation. As I've said before, following Jesus is the only way to undo our bentness. Bible teaching and church family correction, under the authority of Christ and bearing His likeness, help a young person pursue a wise maturity that is not tossed back and forth by crafty peers with their own agenda.

This is what the church is for: to direct you to know Christ so that through Him you can have more direction toward a life worth living. Young people who learn to speak in truth and love in the midst of adults in their community are anchored in truth, which means they are not deceived to do things based on false pressures, expectations, or hopes. They know what's up. They are competent to love, which means they are patient, do not envy, do not boast, and are not proud. They do not dishonor others, are not self-seeking, are not easily angered, and do not keep a record of wrongs.

YOUR ON-GROUND INSTRUCTIONS: CHOOSE YOUR FRIENDS WISELY

During this part of the flight, you can sense that people are dismissing the on-ground instructions. The stewardess might be standing at the front of the plane giving detailed emergency instructions, but everyone is trying to get comfortable, set up their movies, dive into a good book, or read the newspaper. Nobody wants to hear the details of what might happen in the event of an unpleasant plane crash. It must be a frustrating part of the flight for the crew, but it's important. It's mandatory because it's important to cover.

It's like watching one of those get-out-alive or survive-a-catastrophe type shows where the specialist is sitting in a plane giving hints on how to survive in an emergency. He tells you that taking a mental picture of your surroundings, mapping an exit strategy in your mind, and being aware of the emergency devices around you are the keys to survival in any situation. While others will panic and despair in the emergency because they don't know where to start, you will be proactive and utilize all your resources.

So now you've boarded the plane and are looking around to see who's on it from the opposite gender. Is there someone who will befriend you? Is there someone who will be interested in you? At this stage you are determined about a few things:

- You're going to ground yourself in truth.
- You're going to fix your eyes on the life that Jesus offers.
- You're not going to move quickly into anything emotional or physical (girls, you're going to set boundaries; boys, you're going to show self-control).
- You're going to listen to your parents.
- You're going to get involved with a church family.

The last on-ground instruction left is this: *choose your friends wisely*. Peers are important. Some of my closest friends have become lifelong brothers. They are loyal to God. They care for my needs even today. We share history and beliefs and have deep bonds. I would trust them with my life. Our parents still get together, and now we all get together with our spouses and children. It's awesome.

BAD COMPANY CORRUPTS

In 1 Corinthians 15:33, Paul says, "Do not be misled: 'Bad company corrupts good character.'" Don't be deceived: there are those you've invited to join in your aviation journey who will corrupt your good character. They are sitting beside you, around you, in front of you, and in the window seat. They will be loud and obnoxious. They will complain to the cabin staff. They will whine. They will drink. They will flirt. They will seduce. They will cry. They will be immature. You will find yourself doing damage control all the time, but you will also find yourself trapped inflight at 34,000 feet with these hooligans. They will scare off serious young men and women who want to know you. They will undermine your parents' leadership and turn you into what they are if you keep their company long enough.

I will admit that I myself was "bad company." I know of parents who said to their kids, "Stay away from that Michael Thiessen." I say good on them. They loved their kids way more than I did, and they loved them enough to warn them about boys like me. Even though I was offended at the time, I now applaud these parents for warning their kids about me. I had a foul mouth, I was a thief, I lied, I was overly physical with girls, and I was out of control most of the time because of alcohol.

I was nineteen when I realized I didn't want to be that man anymore. And furthermore, I realized the emptiness and falseness of that life. I really wish it weren't so, but some of my buddies were as much of an outright bad influence on me as I was on others. Many times we finagled ourselves into doing things when my conscience told me otherwise, and they didn't share my beliefs in Christ. At the turning point in my life, these guys were fairly entrenched in partying, and I was hungry for something fresh. Jesus said, "What good is it for a man to gain the whole world, yet forfeit his soul?" (Mark 8:36). I knew I needed new heroes and new friends, because the rowdy crowd, whom I previously cheered, was in control of my plane.

New Heroes

In reality, I already had heroes, but I was a bit ashamed of them and didn't want to put into action what they taught. Jesus was, and still is, my biggest hero. At that time, I knew I had to stop being ashamed of His radical teachings and supernatural origins. I believed He came from heaven and offered me forgiveness and full life. Or did I? If I believed, I had to put my full weight on Him. No more tiptoeing onto the elevator. I had to jump in and see if I went up or down. I jumped in, and I went up.

Most of my other heroes were people of faith in history who followed God with conviction. Men like Abraham, Joseph, Moses, David, the Israelite prophets, the apostles of Jesus, Athanasius, Martin Luther, John Bunyan, Dietrich Bonhoeffer, Eric Liddell, Jim Elliot, and Nate Saint. I had always admired their bravery when I heard their stories in church, but I had not yet shared in the experience of their sufferings. These were men of conviction whose resolve had passed the test of opposition. I had not yet known what it would be like to stand out. Did I really admire them? If so, I knew I should be acting more like them by following their examples. No more listening to popular rock idols for my lyrical wisdom. I would trust these solid Christian servants knew something Axle Rose didn't.

It's hard to make Jesus your hero when the people around you mock and reject Him constantly. It's hard to resist corruption when your closest friends are the ones who are encouraging you to do the opposite of what wise old leaders do. Once I put some of my old friends aside and fully trusted Jesus, and once I started following other Christian heroes, I began to grow in wisdom and discipline. The wisdom I found in these heroes created a bedrock on which my life could stand firm, and I have never been the same. Sometimes life is still hard and the ease of comfort still scratches at me, but my body no longer bares the fresh scars of outright rebellion.

NEW FRIENDS

Someone once said, "No man is an island." If you shed some friends, inevitably you will need others. If you empty your cup, you will need to fill it again. Again, at that turning point in my life, I realized I needed new friends who would walk with me and encourage me.

Now, I was a nice kid, I think. I was likeable, I think. But I wasn't wholesome. My old friends were the same as I was. They were nice and likeable, but they weren't wholesome. I don't know if there are any kids who are totally wholesome, but you have to seek out the ones who are trying as much as possible. Proverbs says, "Plans fail for lack of counsel, but with many advisers they succeed.... A man of many companions may come to ruin, but there is a friend who sticks closer than a brother" (15:22; 18:24).

Good friends enrich life. They sit with you on the flight and remind you to behave. They have fun, but within limits. They attract other serious and wise young men and women to you. They are able to relate to you uniquely and yet do not endorse dumping your parents' advice. They have a shared deep culture with you. They are there for you when adversity comes. You will have to be selective and patient to find them. You will have to search them out in Christian environments. But first you will have to lose the idiots.

YOU CAN'T FLY WITHOUT YOUR DOCUMENTS

What if you were standing at the gate, ready to board, and the attendant said, "You don't have your passport and boarding pass, so I can't let you on the plane." There wouldn't be much you could do. You would be stranded.

Well, you and I both know I can't say that. I can't say, "You can't date or court someone until you listen to your parents, accept the church's authority in your life, and lose the idiot friends." In reality, you can do whatever you want. However, that being said, I want to tell you that *you can't court someone until you listen to your parents, accept the church's authority in your life, and lose the idiot friends.* Seriously.

I am currently in the process of watching a young woman pull away from her family, church life, and our Christian fellowship at school for the sake of a new boyfriend. It is painful to watch her change rather than stand firm on the gifts God has given her. I look forward to her shaking this rebellion off, and I highly recommend that you honor your parents and listen to God's people as well. This will give you greater vision to lose the friends that drag you down and choose others of good character.

Six
IN-FLIGHT LOUNGING

WE ARE FINALLY IN THE AIR

I love spy books and movies, particularly the ones in which the main character—like Jason Bourne, Jack Bauer, or James Bond—has to battle against a corrupt government and find out who's behind a huge conspiracy. (Notice the "J.B." conspiracy?)

With each of these characters, the best victories are always conceived even before the villain devises his evil plot. Because the secret agent is so wise, experienced, and strong, he ends up victorious because he has foreseen and planned for the unpredictable actions of his enemy. He is always one step ahead of everyone else. He is one Kung-Fu move ahead of his enemy's punch. He is one gunshot ahead of the other's trigger finger. He might get behind for a moment, but then he thinks of a silver-bullet idea that penetrates the layers of obstacles ahead. In this case, it would a simple solution to get him on the plane of dating safely, even though Dr. Evilton had blocked each concourse with snipers and bombs.

Just like these secret agents, you can prepare for your victorious arrival even before you take off the ground. If you think ahead, believe Scripture, respond to godly authority, and accept Christ's leadership in your life about these matters, you will be far ahead of the rest of the world. Even if you've had some stumbles, you can take these words of encouragement and apply them to yourself to create a silver-bullet pathway to the airplane. In fact, I am confident that you are ready to fly because of the work you've done so far. Now, let's get off the ground and go in-flight lounging.

> FRIENDSHIP: *a state of mutual trust and ongoing support; a person with whom one has a bond of mutual affection.*

FRIENDSHIP ATTRACTION: *When men and women bond emotionally, they also grow in physical attraction toward one another because they generally fulfill their needs for significance in uniquely male and uniquely female ways.*

COURTSHIP: *A deliberate state of mutual trust and ongoing support to determine a person's character, competency, and chemistry with another, while being mindful of the growing physical attraction, and preparing for the possibility of marriage.*

START EVERYTHING LATER

The first rule of engagement is lateness. No, I'm not talking about the time to arrive for drinks. I'm talking about restraining yourselves in a radical way when it comes to the opposite sex. This is "out of this world" for most people. One young lady said to me, "That's unrealistic. Modern parents and students won't do that." However outdated as it sounds, I firmly believe you need to restrain yourself from unintentional friendships and dating until you are mature enough for a serious relationship and ready to be married.

I was driving down a stretch of road that winded its way through farm country toward cottage country. Where I was driving, there was a stretch of highway that was on a long hill. I was going up, and there were solid lines painted on the road so cars wouldn't pass, because drivers couldn't see over the hill. However, I remember how I would routinely pass cars on this road when I was young, even though the lines were as solid as a steel beam.

One particular night, I was driving on that road with a good friend of mine. I had just pulled out to pass a car. I had to downshift into second gear to get the car moving faster. The engine was just screaming. We were in the middle of the pass when a group of vehicles came over the top of the hill. We were barely inching past the car, even with my foot to the floor. The oncoming car started honking. I was terrified. In the end, the car driving beside me slowed down so I could get back in. I veered back into our lane at the last minute.

We almost got into a head-on collision because I was young and impatient. That day I almost killed myself and one of my best friends. Think of this as an illustration for dating without the intention to get married. It's too reckless, too blind, too fast, and too dangerous.

How, then, should you approach dating appropriately? Where do you start?

ESTABLISH A FRIENDSHIP INTENTIONALLY AS GUIDED BY STANDARDS

A "piano standard" is a tune or song that has such an established popularity that it becomes a measure, a norm, and even a model for aspiring musicians. These are songs in which the melody has so much quality and unique technical achievement that it is internationally accepted as a measure of competency for great musicians. You must be able to play these standards to achieve excellence and have them down in order for professionals to accept you as one of them. Young musicians practice these piano scales and guitar rifts time and time again to become the best. Musicians continue to uphold the "standards" of their craft.

In the same way, you need to find a *standard* individual to be your spouse. You should be looking for someone who has quality and excellence. He or she is to be praiseworthy and attract applause. You should be looking for someone who has the three Cs: character, competency, and chemistry.

Many managers use the three Cs as criterion for hiring purposes. It's a common practice, and with a slight alternation to the third C (chemistry), you can use these standards for relationships as well. You should know them, seek to discover someone who will live up to them, and find someone who is at least close to them before you even think about dating. We will look at character and competency first.

Who Is a Standard Guy?

1. Character: he has mental and moral quality
    A. Fears God (Proverbs 1:7, Exodus 1:21)
    B. Loves God and people (Matthew 22:37)
    C. Honest (Proverbs 6:19)
    D. Teachable and humble (Proverbs 8:9; 13:1; 15:20)

E. Kind (Proverbs 11:17)
   F. Generous (Proverbs 11:24, 26; 21:13)
   G. Patient (Proverbs 15:18; 16:32; 19:11)
   H. Self-controlled (Proverbs 25:28), which means he is:
      i) Not violent (Proverbs 3:31; 16:29)
      ii) Not argumentative (Proverbs 26:21)
      iii) Not twisted (Proverbs 3:32; 12:8; 16:28; 28:6)
      iv) Not having transient sexual relationships (Proverbs 6:28–29,32)
2. Competency: he has the ability to complete a task successfully
   A. Hardworking (Proverbs 10:5; 12:14, 27)
   B. Cautious in friendships (Proverbs 12:26; 18:24; 1 Corinthians 15:33)
   C. Prudent in business (Proverbs 14:15; 20:25; 22:24–27)
   D. Discerning (Proverbs 3:13)
   E. Faithful—loyal, constant, and steady (Proverbs 14:14; 16:6; 28:20)
   F. Skillful in his work (Proverbs 22:29)
   G. Ready to actively and sacrificially love a wife (Ephesians 5:25–28)
   H. Ready to actively lead his children (Ephesians 6:4)

WHO IS A STANDARD GIRL?

1. Character: she has mental and moral quality
   A. Fears God (Proverbs 1:7; 15:33; 31:30)
   B. Loves God and people (Matthew 22:37)
   C. Modest (Proverbs 6:20; 1 Timothy 2:19)
   D. Noble—has personal and moral quality (Proverbs 12:4; 31:10, 25)
   E. Gentle (Proverbs 25:15; 1 Peter 3:4; 1 Thessalonians 2:7)
   F. Kind (1 Peter 3:4)
   G. Generous (Proverbs 31:20)
   H. Patient (Proverbs 15:18; 16:32; 19:11)

I. Self-Controlled (Proverbs 25:28; Titus 2:5), which means she is:
   i) Not argumentative (Proverbs 19:13; 21:9,19; 25:24)
   ii) Not seductive to other men (Proverbs 2:16, 20)
   iii) Not even suggestive to other men (Proverbs 6:24)
2. Competency: she has the ability to complete a task successfully
   A. Hard working (Proverbs 31:13-15,17, 27)
   B. Attentive to her family's needs (Proverbs 31:15, 28; Titus 2:4)
   C. Able to manage a home and estate (Proverbs 31:15,16,18, 21–22, 27; Titus 2:4–5)
   D. Ready to actively and submissively love a husband (Ephesians 5:22)
   E. Ready to actively care for children (Titus 2:4)

Now, I am a list guy. There is a lot of information in these lists and a lot to take in at a glance. They are formatted so you can spend time looking at the Bible references and meditating on each point. You have to understand them and interpret them according the Bible, which takes a bit of time. However, the scriptures speak for themselves on these things. These attributes regarding character and competency describe the "wise man" and the "woman worth more than rubies." You want to find one of these individuals.

Here is the key: I suggest you find out all of these things *without* dating. You can find the wise man or the valuable woman without entering into a dating relationship at all. You don't need to date someone to get to know his or her character and see if he or she is competent. You can get to know those things within a good friendship if you start with intentional thinking, asking the right questions, and watching the person in certain situations.

Let's redeem the word "standard." You are not looking for someone who will just help you get by. You are looking for excellence and praiseworthiness in character and competency. You start with standards, then ask the right questions, then observe the individual in multiple settings, then ask others whom you trust (including your parents) what they think, and then you go back to the individual and tell him or her what you've observed.

When you've told that person what your parents and mentors think, you have the opportunity to watch his or her reaction, interpret the response, and then ask yourself, *Who is this individual as I have truly come to know him or her?* Many people are surprised when the person reacts immaturely to some honest criticism. It sounds cold and calculated, because it is void of romance at this stage. That's okay. All these actions are to be done without any physical contact and with minimal emotional investment, because you are just looking, not tasting.

I have a rule with my kids when we go shopping. I always say, "We look with our eyes, not with our hands." When we are in the store, there are things available for purchase all around us. I don't expect my kids to close their eyes to everything. Except in certain sections, they are allowed to see what is in front of them. They are allowed to ask me questions ("How's it made? What's it made of? How does it work?"). I am actually pleased when my children try to understand what's good or bad about the products in the store—when they try to find the standard ingredients for which we are all looking. However, they are not allowed to pick it up or put it in their mouth. They are not allowed to touch or taste anything.

Getting to know someone is much like our family shopping experience. The idea is to get to know the other person and become familiar enough with him or her to see if that person suits your needs. But remember, this process does not require touching or tasting at all. There can only be so much "getting to know each other" in this phase, or else damage ensues for all. So look for a standard person. Know what ingredients make up a wise man or valuable woman. But don't pick that person up or put him or her in your mouth.

There are many practical ways to have intentional friendships without dating. Here are a few suggestions: (1) spend time with the individual in group settings, without any alcoholic consumption to dilute the situation; (2) keep time spent alone limited to public settings, and arrive and leave separately; (3) don't travel together alone; (4) don't do anything physical; and (5) state your intentions and standards clearly if the issue of dating or romance arises.

LIMIT THE FUEL AND DECREASE THE BURN TIME

I am referring to this idea of being involved romantically with the intention of marriage as "courting." You may still use the word "dating." What I'm saying is that you shouldn't date/court until you are ready to work toward a marriage with someone. Don't cross the line from being in a friendship to being in a relationship until you have mentally accepted the responsibility to journey toward marriage with that person. You should be ready and be committed to set marriage on the horizon.

In order to make the dating stage of the relationship play its role—and it does have a role—you have to understand the difference between "dating with the intention to get married" and "taste-and-see dating." When you have a friendship and you're considering marriage as a possibility, it makes a huge difference in your lounging attitude and actions when you take the step into dating.

The Second Law of Thermodynamics states "entropy in a reaction always increases." This means that when you add energy or fuel to a chemical reaction, the randomness always increases. For example, if you add wood or oxygen to a burning fire, the flame increases and the wood burns more rapidly. If you heat a kettle of water, the molecules move more rapidly until they disperse into steam. If you fly a plane into a mountain at a high velocity, the crash shatters the fuselage. This is a consistent physical law.

I propose that relationships have a similar law that consistently governs them as well: *sexual appetite in an individual who is dating always increases.* This is often how we crash the plane. This is how we let the fire burn uncontrollably. This is why danger ensues in the cabin of the plane. When people date without the intention of getting married, they are only doing so to experiment physically and emotionally, without any goals or controls. Boys want friendship and sex. Girls want friendship and companionship.

When a boy asks out a girl, he may like her as a friend, but now he is revealing he also wants to play with her body in some form or another. When a girl asks out a boy, she is revealing her desire to be exclusively with him and to be cherished above all others. She wants to become more intimate with him. As I've already established, friendship attraction is real, which means any form of dating multiplies the draw in people to doing both physical and emotional things together. Dating creates intimacy, intimacy in the relationship always increases, and as intimacy increases sexual desire stirs. If someone is dating without any intention to get married to a standard individual, all that is achieved is adding fuel to an already almost uncontrollable fire.

Although most of our culture believes this premature "experimenting" and "test-driving" is good, I consider it to be a problem. People have bought into the lie that dating is the process in which we taste. They think dating is similar to going to the market and trying out a bit of everything before you buy. They pick up the fruit and take a bite. They smell some of the cheeses and take a nibble. They drink the different soda pops and then put the bottle back on the shelf. This is how they try to figure out what they like. It is an error.

This kind of feeding only leads to gluttony, addictive eating, and addictive sexuality void of permanence and meaning. If we go into a dating relationship with the mindset that "we're just tasting," we will move on to the next person once we've achieved our goal "to taste." Girls say, "I'm tasting to see if this is the kind of guy I like emotionally. It is! Great! I can't really commit right now, but I'll have sex to keep him around for now, and maybe I'll end up looking for this kind of guy later." Guys say, "I'm tasting to see if this is what I like sexually. It is. Great! I'll just keep her for a while because she makes me feel significant, but I will move on because I'm not ready for anything permanent." If you are too young to commit, don't experiment.

In this type of dating, you've already had some form of a meal. In fact, you're fat, so to speak, because you've had many meals. Your objective has been accomplished, even though you have no long-term plan or control. You taste, fill up, move on, taste again, fill up again, and move on because of the way you've approached the situation. This form of dating doesn't provide long-lasting significance. Rather, it offers a stomachache or heart burn.

This type of dating feeds sexual appetites until they are uncontrollable. Young men want sex here and now, then and there, all the time, anywhere, with any girl who will make them feel significant. Young women want companionship now, at all physical costs, with any guy who makes them feel cherished. We magnify the force of the physical draw toward another person one-thousand fold when we start playing "man and wife."

Whether you are sixteen or twenty, if you don't plan on getting married soon, or if you are incapable of becoming engaged in the near future, then don't put yourself in intimate and physical "dating" situations. I can't overstate this enough. Sexual appetite in an individual who is dating always increases.

Think of it this way. If you hold hands when you're fourteen, you will immediately hold hands and do something more when you're fifteen. If you hold hands and kiss when you are fifteen, you will naturally hold hands, kiss, and do something more when you're sixteen. When you turn seventeen, you immediately hold hands, kiss, grope, touch, and then engage in *something more*. If you've already engaged in physical activities in a relationship, when you break up and move to the next person, you will rush to that physical point.

Do you see the progression? It happens so quickly. You can go from holding hands to oral sex in a matter of a few short relationships. Sometimes this progression happens over a few years, and sometimes it occurs all in one night. It depends how reckless you are. Once you feed your sexual appetite, it is impossible to shut it down or put it off.

Let's assume you plan to go to college. Let's also assume you don't plan to get married until you've graduated. If that is the case, if you're sixteen years old now, the earliest point in which you would potentially get married is most likely eight years away, at age twenty-four. If you start dating now with no intention of getting married until you're twenty-four, that's eight years of tasting and seeing without any higher goals or controls.

Let's say your plan is to remain pure until marriage. That's eight years of experimenting right at the line while trying not to cross it. This is unnatural and unrealistic. It's like saying to someone, "Hey, let's experiment with explosives in our laps for eight years, pile on the fuel, and ignore the properties of nature. I bet we won't get blown up." Proverbs 6:27 says, "Can a man scoop fire into his lap without his clothes being burned?"

Let's say you currently don't care about being pure. That's eight years of experimenting and trying not to feel the consequences of those actions. It's like saying to someone, "Let's sit in the garage with the car running for eight years and try not to get any fumes in our mouths." Proverbs 6:28 says, "Can someone walk on hot coals without their feet being scorched?"

Being in the dating scene for eight years makes it impossible for you to be pure for marriage. If you start dating when you're too young (anytime before being serious about marriage commitment), the experiment will be too explosive, the fire too wild, to survive. You will fall into despair. Again, sexual appetite in an individual who is dating always increases.

You cannot start being intimate in little bits with the opposite sex at a young age and expect to remain pure for long. You will explore new experiences, but you won't be able to protect love. It will slip away from you because you are not pursuing it—you are just pursuing a play version of it. You will only get baggage, and you will regret those experiences when your spouse looks into your eyes and says, "I can't believe you did that so many times. I can't believe you did it in so many places. Am I not special?"

Some spouses may never say these things, because they are full of confusion. Those might be even more explosive situations. In either case, you will regret past experiences when the one you love doesn't want to relive them with you because you've violated trust. You might ask, "How can prior experiences break this trust?" Because God designed sex to be between a husband and wife, not shared around the bar.

Don't be intimate, and don't tempt your appetite until you are preparing for marriage. By waiting until a later time to be romantically inclined with one particular individual, you have starved the fuel of the fire by limiting the times you stir sexual desires. If you start dating when you are serious and ready for marriage, you make survival doable.

Young women, this means you don't start dating until you're ready to be a mother, ready to be busy in your home, ready to be a helpmate to a husband, ready to submit your body to fulfill his sexual needs, and ready to be faithful even when life is hard and difficult (see Ephesians 5; Titus 3). Some of these things may not be your current goals, but they are the responsibilities that come along with sex. This doesn't mean you start dating when you think you're ready to enjoy friendships with boys alone. It is an entirely different thing.

Young men, this means you don't start dating until you're ready to provide for a young wife, ready to commit to her, ready to sacrifice for her as you would for your own body, and ready to be a good friend by placing her friendship above all other friendships (see Ephesians 5; 1 Timothy 5:8). Some of these ideas may seem chauvinistic in our culture, but God has established them so we men can bless women. As Paul says, "If anyone does not provide for his relatives, and especially for his immediate family, he has denied the faith." This doesn't mean you start dating when you think you're ready to enjoy sex. It is an entirely different thing.

I got my license at the young age of sixteen. Currently, though, young drivers in Canada have to wait a few years later to get their full license. There is a longer learning process, which includes greater supervision and less freedom. Our government has standards and forces our young people to become a little older and wiser before it allows them to drive. Maybe as a result there will be fewer young men pulling out into oncoming traffic as they race to the cottage. Perhaps there will be fewer immature and foolish young people who put their lives, and the lives of others, in jeopardy.

This is what I'm saying with dating. If you don't start dating until you're ready for marriage, it's likely you won't be as reckless because you will be a little more mature and wiser. You won't want to "play marriage." You will be closer to the point of being able to bear the responsibilities and enjoy the privileges of real marriage.

CHARACTER, COMPETENCY, AND CHEMISTRY DETERMINES READINESS

When people date before they have the intention to get married, it leads to disaster. However, even when people date *with* the intention to get married, sexual appetite still increases, even though they are not just experimenting. The wisest man with the highest standards will still have growing sexual desires. The most virtuous woman will want to explore the joys of intimacy as she trusts him more. Up until this point, we've only discussed starving this appetite. Now we need to discuss another way to deal with it: by getting married and satisfying your appetite in a secure and significant marriage relationship.

Our culture promotes two lies: (1) it is good for young people to date aimlessly to "taste and see," and (2) young adults shouldn't get married. It tells young people, "Taste, see, touch, but don't commit. Just have fun, and don't think about the future. Get yourself established in a career, but not in a home. Travel the world and see all the beaches now instead of sharing these experiences with your young spouse. Get all your schooling and fun done, and then settle down." The world tells us to do all these things before even considering marriage. That is a recipe for disaster. One does not rob, pillage, and steal in order to become an honest and hard-working man. We might as well train ourselves to swing a golf club left-handed even though we are a right-handed shooter.

You must overcome these lies. While I don't want you to start dating young and then marry in foolishness, the opposite is also not good. Therefore, once you've found a standard person, at a time when you have character and competency to support yourselves reasonably, get on with adulthood. Seal and protect your love with the commitment of marriage vows.

LIVING TOGETHER DOESN'T COUNT

In high school, I had a friend who always waited until the last minute to decide whether he would join us for a night out. He would always look around for other people to see if there was something better to do. He wouldn't choose us first, just because we were his best friends. This always left me feeling like a second choice. I would say, "Are we not good enough to be your first choice? Are we not good enough for you to commit to us earlier in the day?"

This is the way I feel about living together. It is playing marriage, but the individuals aren't actually willing to choose one another. It is just a more complex stage of the "tasting and touching" process. People want the convenience of living together so they can have sex and share expenses. They want to live together to eliminate other possible suitors. But at the end of the day, they are still just lounging on the plane. They haven't arrived anywhere. They are still looking around for better options to "make certain" they have the right one. Living together is not marriage. It doesn't count. It is void of the powerful aspects of marriage.

If I could boil marriage down, the sugary maple syrup sweetness of it would be three things: marriage is consecration, consummation, and ongoing commitment. Nothing less. These three things make marriage powerful and rich beyond our human understanding. Anything else is a fraud.

Consecration

Marriage begins with consecration. Consecration is the act of declaring something sacred by regarding it with great respect. Jesus taught, "Haven't you read…that at the beginning the Creator 'made them male and female,' and said, 'For this reason a man will leave his father and mother and be united to his wife, and the two will become one flesh'? So they are no longer two, but one. Therefore what God has joined together, let man not separate" (Matthew 19:4–6).

God is the one who brings people together in marriage. He established this kind of relationship in which one person formally dedicates to another with the intention of fulfilling a promise. This occurs when a man stands in front of God and witnesses to declare his active loyal love: "I will be here. I will remain here. Until death separates us." This occurs when a woman stands in front of God and witnesses to declare her active loyal love: "I am yours, yours alone, body and soul. Until death separates us." Whatever God brings together should stay together. This is why marriage is sacred.

When you consecrate all your energies toward this one purposeful relationship, you are doing something godly, powerful, and full of true love. When two people consecrate themselves to one another in this way before God and other witnesses, they establish a bond of trust that strengthens their grip on one another. They are making an agreement to protect and support each another even when there is strain on the relationship. They are covenanting (which means to cut a deal) before God, and this binds them to one another. It has nobility and sincerity written all over it. It fosters security and creates a foundation for building a stable life. This type of union is not found in common places, for there is nothing common about it.

Living together is nothing like this. In fact, if anything, living together is an agreed-upon non-commitment. That type of union is common. It falls under common law because there is no declared loyalty in it. Do you know what "common law" means? It is the part of English law derived from custom and judicial precedent rather than agreements or statutes. It is law that has been adopted and modified through previous disputes rather than written contracts.

When a partner in a long-term relationship of cohabitation files for separation, there is no agreement for the lawyers to see. They have to study what other disputes have occurred and how those were handled. The relationship is defined by an unimpressive list of ways to divvy stuff up. Living by common law is below standard. Where is the sacred loyalty? Where is the active love? It is just a plan to take a car for a test drive with no intention of buying it. It's deciding to be a taste-tester but not committing to a meal. It's getting a guest pass into a lab so you can play with the chemicals without taking any responsibility if things go bad.

Consummation

Consummation is the point at which something is complete or finalized. For example, in a sale, consummation occurs when money is exchanged for a product. Both the seller and the buyer know that something has been completed. In marriage, consummation is the action of making it complete by having sexual intercourse. We've already discovered that God designed sex to bind the husband and wife together. It is the process by which two things become one: two families become one as the union binds them together; two individuals become one as their bodies fit together; two fluids become one to make conception of a new generation possible.

Sex is intended to complete the sacred agreement of marriage. Both parties understand what's happened and what's been agreed upon. "When I give this to you, you give me something back. When I give something to you, you give me that back." For the woman, she knows the man has committed himself to her, so in exchange she gives her body to him. For the man, he knows the woman has given her body to him, so in exchange he binds himself with loyalty to her alone until death separates them.

The night of consummation is intended to be a stamped seal on the act of consecration. Just as a person dips a signet ring into hot wax to make a seal, so two lovers make a passionate and permanent imprint on one another. Through this act they say, "We declared it, we've sealed it, and now it will remain unbroken." It is a physical reminder of their dedication, filled with taste, touch, sight, sound, and smell. This act re-enforces their unity and de-programs their individuality.

In the Bible, an example of consummation is found in the marriage of Isaac and Rebekah. In this story, Abraham asks a servant to search for a wife for his son, Isaac. The servant goes to a local water well, where young women would draw water. There he comes across Rebekah, who is filling a large jar for her household. She is a beautiful virgin with a gentle spirit, and she reveals that she wants to marry Isaac. Her family immediately releases her to go and be married, and she and the servant return to Isaac. This is how they become married: "Isaac brought her into the tent of Sarah his mother, and he took Rebekah, and she became his wife, and he loved her. So Isaac was comforted after his mother's death" (Genesis 24:67).

We have to unravel some of the details to understand this story. First, "the tent of Sarah his mother" is a general reference to the large nomadic tent that Sarah's descendants inhabited. It would have been full of rooms and separations. By this time Isaac's mother was already dead, and Rebekah was moving from her family tent into the family tent of Isaac. It was as if Isaac was bringing Rebekah into a small hotel on the night of the wedding where the rest of the family was also staying. It would have made the appropriate sacred public statement, but the couple would have had the appropriate privacy.

"He took Rebekah" is a statement about sex. We could say, "Isaac swept her off her feet, and they took hold of each other." It is clear they had sexual intercourse. By this act, "she became his wife." Their public entrance into the tent, along with their physical union, sealed the covenant. Sex finalized the sacred situation, and there was no going back after that event. It was at this moment that Rebekah became "his wife."

Because of this, Isaac "loved her." Now, we don't get to hear about Rebekah's feelings, but it's clear that Isaac found significant meaning in this act of making love. He felt a comfort that even overpowered his grief after his mother's death. He was free from restraint and put at ease. The words "he loved her" have many different nuances that add meaning to the expression: "he liked her; he befriended her; he panted after her; he become her lover; he had a deep romantic and sexual attachment to her; he had intense feelings for her."

When sex occurs before marriage, it is like a buyer handing over the money before a deal has been made, or a seller handing over the merchandise too quickly. What would happen if the seller held back the merchandise after receiving payment? What would happen if the buyer held back payment after receiving the goods? In each case, something that was intended to finalize the deal would evolve into a hurtful dispute and undermine the ongoing relationship. Premarital sex does this to relationships. Living together undermines relationships. It is a short-change version of the real thing that doesn't seal anything. One person is always left feeling gypped, and neither truly feels secure. People are left asking, "Did I get it right enough yet? Am I good enough yet? Will he ever deliver? Isn't my body satisfying him?"

Ongoing Commitment

The cement of a relationship is ongoing commitment. This commitment must last until death parts the two individuals. It is being dedicated, engaged, and obligated to stay firm for all life. We build foundations for homes with cement. We build bridges to span long distances with steel. We pave roads for high access with cement. Ongoing commitment is the strong bonding agent we need for relationships.

Do you remember saying "my dad can fix anything" when you were a kid? If a sword hilt splintered, or a plastic gun snapped, or a paper project ripped, your dad could engineer a solution for it. It was amazing what some metal and glue could do. My dad could twist metal wiring and apply hot glue to repair most of my toys. It was great.

Do you remember trying to fix a toy yourself? Do you remember the frustration? Most likely, you couldn't do it at all. Most likely, your work fell apart quickly. Kids try to hold a hockey stick together with scotch tape. They don't understand structural design. They don't understand proper reinforcement. They don't understand weight-bearing issues. They don't understand the power of leverage. So they tape things that need glue and steel.

Think of relationships as foundations, bridges, and roads. Every relationship is exposed to stress, conflict, and trauma. Everyday usage makes certain the inevitably of brokenness. There are cracks or splinters. There are punctures and holes. There is ongoing pressure. Every relationship needs to be built with strength to endure. Unfortunately, people who live together are like children trying to hold these fragile relationships together with tape, when what is really required is the strong steel and cement of ongoing commitment within marriage.

One kind of "tape" people try to apply is *perfection*.

Because guys are visually and physically stimulated, they will focus most of their passion to please and be pleased on perfecting both those areas. If there is a problem, they will try to fix it by bettering their appearance and physical experiences. They will try to hold things together by getting everything perfect romantically. "If we desire each other all the time, that will be enough. If we fix all the physical problems, then we will definitely be satisfied."

Because girls are relationally driven, they will focus their passion to please and be pleased by perfecting that area. If there is a problem, they will want to fix it by spending more time together, communicating more, and reducing conflict.

So, there will be two different pushes, until the relationship becomes a constant push toward these perfections: "Our bodies must be perfect; our sex must be perfect; our income must be perfect; our home must be perfect; our communication must be perfect; our reputation must be perfect; our toys must be perfect." This is hogwash. It's like putting effort into trying to keep a chicken coop clean.

I love the line from the movie *Ever After* where a maid says, "The only throne I want her sitting on is the one I clean everyday." The maid is speaking of a beautiful woman who is also a tyrant. She doesn't want her to be queen. In this expression, the maid humanizes her as if to say, "I know what she smells like, publicly and privately. Even beautiful people use the toilet. She's nothing special. Her poop still stinks."

This is not a pleasant thought, but it's true. Everyone suffers from morning breath. Life is not perfect. It is not all bubble baths and oil massages. So this drive to be perfect just leads to guilt, shame, and hiding ourselves. Women feel they can never live up to a man's sexual expectations or establish a greater vision for life outside of his constant pursuit of perfection. Men feel guilt and shame because they can't keep up, hold it all together, and do it all.

When people live together, they also apply the tape of *foreknowledge*.

"We will get to know everything about each other before we marry, and then we will stay together." They try to find out everything they can about a person. They try to see into the future. This is an attempt to know the impossible—an attempt to see into a future that is unseen.

There is no way to know *all* things about an individual prior to marriage. We can't know if the person will please us sexually now and always. We can't know if the person will continue to please us emotionally now and always. Some great lovers will develop a disease or struggle with fatigue during the parenting years. Some great listeners will become stressed by work or introverted because of the relentless busy pace of life. If we ever hope to establish a relationship full of meaning and purpose, it will require faith and flexibility on our part as we encounter change and difficulties. We shouldn't try to know everything, because commitment holds firm regardless of the unknowns.

Life happens, and things change. The only thing strong enough to withstand all the stress, strain, and seduction of the world is ongoing commitment. If consecration is the initial foundation, then ongoing commitment is the structure or frame of the building. As Malachi 3:15 says, "Has not the LORD made them one? In flesh and spirit they are his. And why one? Because he was seeking godly offspring. So guard yourself in your spirit, and do not break faith with the wife of your youth." Proverbs 5:15-23 says:

> Drink water from your own cistern, running water from your own well. Should your springs overflow in the streets, your streams of water in the public squares? Let them be yours alone, never to be shared with strangers. May your fountain be blessed, and may you rejoice in the wife of your youth. A loving doe, a graceful deer—may her breasts satisfy you always, may you ever be captivated by

her love. Why be captivated, my son, by an adulteress? Why embrace the bosom of another man's wife? For a man's ways are in full view of the LORD, and he examines all his paths. The evil deeds of a wicked man ensnare him; the cords of his sin hold him fast. He will die for lack of discipline, led astray by his own great folly.

Living together is a kind of folly. It is purely sexual and convenient and accomplishes nothing in regard to true commitment. It is applying tape where cement and steel are needed.

Girls, imagine sitting on a plane beside someone of interest, but he keeps scanning the plane for someone better looking or more flirtatious, or he keeps asking you to change your appearance and personality. At some point you would say, "Am I not good enough to be your first choice? Am I not good enough to have your full attention? How long will it be before you figure out there isn't anyone out there better for you?"

Guys, imagine sitting on the plane beside someone of interest, but she keeps listening for a better conversation or for someone with a first-class seat open beside him. At some point you would say, "Is there someone else listening to you? Is there someone else being attentive to you right now? How long will I have to pine away before you realize that I am thoughtful of you and good for you?"

GETTING MARRIED RELEASES UNDUE STRAIN

Strain develops when internal or external forces make severe or excessive demands on something. Gale-force winds put strain on a main sail. Rising and falling seas put strain on the hull of a ship. Crashing waves put strain on sailors. We know dating creates intimacy, and as intimacy increases, sexual desire stirs. This puts serious strain on young people.

Undue strain is the kind of stress that is unnecessary. If we don't sail in the storm, the ship won't become stressed. If we get through the storm quickly, the ship won't be torn apart. Some people lay awake all night worrying about situations they can't change. Some people work out too often to overcome insecurity. Other people overeat to comfort themselves. These situations create stress that can be easily avoided. They place "undue strain" on an individual. In the same way, both taste-and-see-dating and living together put undue strain on people. They create real pressure, but they do not allow for a true, meaningful, release.

Three Groups

So, how can we overcome the undue strain placed on young courting/dating couples? For this, we must go back to the Bible. The apostle Paul is very clear that there is a general human need for us to "get married" so we can feed our sexual appetites in an appropriate way. He writes:

> Now for the matters you wrote about: It is good for a man not to have sexual relations with a woman. But because of the sexual urges, each man should have his own wife, and each woman her own husband. The husband should fulfill his marital duty to his wife, and likewise the wife to her husband. The wife's body does not belong to her alone but also to her husband. In the same way, the husband's body does not belong to him alone but also to his wife.... Each has his own gift from God, one of one kind and one of another. To the unmarried and the widows I say that it is good for them to remain single as I am. But if they cannot exercise self-control, they should marry. For it is better to marry than to burn with passion (1 Corinthians 7:1-4, 7–9).

In this passage, the apostle Paul is making two points. First, if we can remain single in order to devote all our time to the ministry of God, our interests will not be divided and we will serve God by our unique devotion of time. However, if celibacy is not our gift, we should get married in order to release the strain of our growing sexual appetite. Both are acceptable before God. His main priority is our purity.

Paul is writing here to the church in Corinth. Like most cities today, Corinth was full of explicitness and license. Divorce was common. Homosexuality was rampant. Sex outside of marriage was also common, as slave owners mated slaves, the wealthy had concubines or employed prostitutes, temple priestesses promoted sexual veneration of pagan gods, and people lived in the common-law arrangements of the day. Just like today, those who had come to know Jesus had questions about sexuality. We see this when Paul writes, "Now for the matters you wrote about." Jesus formerly taught about the subject briefly and broadly, but Paul now had to teach about this broken reality with specific instructions to help this church.

Some of the believers' questions would have centered around divorce and remarriage, while others would have focused on sex and marriage. Was marriage okay, or should they be celibate? If their pagan friends enjoyed sex, was it permissible for them to enjoy it as well? What forms of sex were permissible for Christians? Should those who were married before they knew Jesus get divorced so they could give all their attention to God? Should young people, the unmarried, or widows get married at all, or should they remain single?

Based on Paul's responses, it appears there were three different groups in the church. The first was comprised of men and women who weren't romantically inclined and didn't feel a strong pull to have sex. These individuals had self-control and could stay pure without having sex. Paul was spearheading a church-planting ministry, and he knew this group could serve as valuable missionaries to the Roman Empire. Their relational freedom could translate into ministry service and devoted sacrifice. They could do things married people could not.

Of course, some people would admire this "grade A" group so much that they would want to engraft the entire church to a strict celibacy. It would only make sense in an over-sexed society that people would esteem those who resisted sexual contact completely. However, as some of these men and women spent time doing meaningful ministry together, it is likely that many of them started to feel pulled toward marriage because of their friendship attraction. What should they do now? Was it okay to marry in the midst of ministry training and service?

I can remember my first and second years of Bible College. Many people would set out with such goals of using their singleness for God, but then they would get interested in someone of the opposite sex and change course. They really struggled between their goals for singleness and the pull of their physical passions. Paul answers, "B+ is a satisfactory missionary grade." He commands this second group to get married in order to remain pure. Marriage does not make them any less of a Christian servant. Purity is more important than time devotion.

The third group in Corinth represented the vast majority of the people in the church. They had always been interested in friendship and sex, even as they desired to serve Christ. (I would have fit tightly into this group.) These individuals were coming from both healthy and broken homes, with vastly different sexual heritages, and did not at all feel the desire to be single. They did not have the self-control to stay pure outside of marriage. They needed a spouse who would be a ministry partner and a sexual outlet.

These men and women had encountered friendship attraction and strong sexual desires early in life. They had hoped to create homes and establish community churches. They wanted to nurture the next generation to join the church and society. What should they do? Should they fight their impulses in order to be celibate? Paul again answers, "B+ is an okay missionary grade." He commands them to get married in order to remain pure. This does not make them any less of a Christian servant. Purity is more important than time devotion.

Today, we find these same three groups in the church. There are those who *remain single* throughout their lifetime in order to serve God. Paul says this is good, if they remain pure. Then there are those who try *singleness for a time*, but then want to get married. Paul says this is good too, if they remain pure. And then there are those who *never want to be single*. Not even for a brief moment. Paul says this is also good, if they remain pure. In fact, each of these cases is acceptable as long as the individual remains pure. One must always put purity before other good pursuits.

PURITY FIRST

This is such an important concept for us today, because our culture puts so many things *before* purity. In our global secular economic market, many voices cry out for our young adults to be fully devoted to their careers first and foremost. Whether in the competitive job market of mainland China or the corporate climate of Toronto, young people are expected to give it all for their jobs. People's status is often defined by their A+ mark on the job, and employers don't naturally accept B+. People's stability is often defined by the size of their bank account.

Gone is the axiom, "We work to live, not live to work." With all our wealth in the Western world, many voices are also encouraging our young people to travel and pursue leisure. "Enjoy life and then settle down," they say. "Marriage is the last piece of the puzzle." This might work for those who can remain single throughout their lifetime. It might even work somewhat for those who try singleness for a time. But it is devastating for the majority of young people who never want to be single because of friendship attraction, maleness and femaleness, and sexual appetite.

Our young people are living with undue strain. They are living with unnecessary pressure because they aren't given permission to marry young. They are receiving pressure from society to have sex young but to get married late and pursue material wealth. According to Scripture, if the tasks of ministry fall second to purity, the other material pursuits will fall even shorter. They will have lesser meaning and offer lesser benefits.

Don't get me wrong; there are some tasks we cannot avoid. I do agree that young men and women need to prepare for their future. Each person has to grow up and survive in the world. But it's not healthy to place so much emphasis on wealth accumulation and individualism. Young married couples, even where a young mom can stay at home, are capable of surviving the same as anyone else. It just requires principles and planning. They have to make purity their first priority and then work toward the other things. Jesus said something specific about this when He told us, "Seek first his kingdom and his righteousness, and all these things will be given to you as well. Therefore do not worry about tomorrow, for tomorrow will worry about itself. Each day has enough trouble of its own" (Matthew 6:33–34).

The Bible makes it clear that purity comes before either ministry or stability. If ministry is subject to one's gifts and self-control, how much more should these lesser things be as well? If Paul can say, "Get married even if it lessens your ministry effectiveness," how much more can we say, "Get married even if it affects your career or travel plans"? Purity is more important than ministry and much more important than financial stability and travel.

So many people have this mixed up. They ask young adults to remain detached to some things but promote full attachment to other things. As two young adults grow closer together, people ask them to publicly deny the pull toward marriage while secretly promoting them to burn with passion. They encourage them to put off purity to pursue these lesser things.

This is topsy-turvy to Scripture. God puts purity first. It is the first piece of the puzzle. When it is placed first, all the other pieces can then be put into place to form a great picture. When it doesn't come first, it puts undue strain on young men and women because they try to force things. Have you ever watched toddlers try to force a puzzle together? They get so frustrated because nothing fits and the grander picture is a mess. In the same way, young men and women are finding stress and frustration as they taste-and-see date and live together.

Undue Strain

In his letter to the Corinthians, Paul builds on this idea of marriage to address those who were already in relationships. He writes, "If anyone thinks that he is not behaving in a pure way toward his girlfriend, if it is a matter of undue strain and he feels he ought to marry, he should do what he wishes. There is no sin: let them get married" (1 Corinthians 7:36, my translation).

The Greek word translated as "not behaving in a pure way" literally means "he is being rude, shameful, or indecent." So if a man is promoting forbidden sexual acts or entertaining such explicit thoughts, and is therefore causing dishonor to his girlfriend, it is indecent and the two should get married to solve the problem. If he is being convicted about his lack of purity toward her, the two should get married in order to consecrate and consummate the relationship, which will aid their ongoing commitment.

The word translated as "girlfriend" literally means "his young woman or his girl." She is either his girlfriend or is actually his fiancée. In either case, two things are clear: they are in a relationship, and he is feeling impure.

The phrase "if it is a matter of undue strain" could mean two different things because the phrase has no gender. It could be referring to the stage of life of the girlfriend, or it might be referring to the passions of the young man.

In the first case, it would be applied to the girlfriend's age or stage of life, which would mean, "if she is past the flower of her youth," or "if she is past her prime," or "if she is past the highest point of a young woman's development." With this in mind, it would certainly be referring to the woman who is feeling anxious about wasting her childbearing years. This might refer to a younger but more mature woman, or it might refer to a woman who is aging. Either way, the woman is ready to be married and waiting for the man to make a commitment.

In the second case, "undue strain" could refer to the man's intensity of feelings or passions. Several translators render it "if his passions are strong," or "if his sexual appetite is too hungry." In this case it refers to his need to have sex to feel significant. He has brushed close to this woman, and now it is completely unrealistic for him to go on without doing something more physical.

I prefer the wider translation of the *ESV* because it includes both possibilities. It is natural for women to want to plan for a home and children. Many women have a strong desire early in life to bear children and develop a family. This isn't always the case, but it is the norm. Does the man's situation sound normal too? His sexual appetite is strong. No shock there. Thus, if a man has a girlfriend and there is a mutual pull that has become counterproductive to purity, it is better for the couple to marry than to try to sustain the pretense of detachment.[1]

In both cases, the strain is "undue" because it can be easily resolved by marriage. For the woman, the ongoing stress is unnecessary because she wants to establish a home and is sexually interested in her betrothed, so she should be a willing partner in marriage. For the man, the ongoing stress is unnecessary because he wants sex, he has already established the relationship, and they already have chemistry, so he should be a willing partner in marriage. When the pull of passion or attraction goes beyond reasonable limits, if there are no moral red flags to stop the relationship (as the text says, "and it is the right thing"), marriage releases undue strain to solve both problems.[2] This makes the relationship sacred. It is a plan for sexual release that also keeps the home in mind. It fosters ongoing commitment.

Marriage is the only relationship that takes into account the needs of both the man and the woman. It is hard work, full of struggle and victory. But by its very nature it also takes into consideration both sexes. It is a battle *for* the sexes rather than a battle *of* the sexes.

When you develop character and competence, find a standard person who also possesses these traits, and sense the pull of passion or attraction beyond reasonable limits, you should get married! It is unnecessary for you to hold back for the sake of ministry, stability, or the cultural pressure to be *A+* in the eyes of the world. You should move forward with consecration, consummation, and ongoing commitment, because purity is so important to God. He promises that if you obey Him, He will provide for your needs.

CHRISTIANS MARRY CHRISTIANS, PERIOD

If you are reading this book, you are either a follower of Jesus or are hearing some advice from an outside Christian perspective. I appreciate both audiences. Thanks for reading along.

But if you are a follower of Christ, this section is particularly important for you. It is important because God has given you a clear command regarding *whom* you should marry. My hope is that this book will illuminate your mind from God's perspective, but this section bears His authority with certainty. This is what it means to have God tell you what to do. Dear brother, dear sister, let Him guide you now. You must make decisions that are pleasing to Jesus, your resurrected King. He died and rose again on the third day so you might have eternal life. He died to pay for your sins. He rose again because He has power over death. Now He reigns as your spiritual king, and His commands affect every bit of your life.

If you are not a follower of Jesus, read this section as a critical realist. This material is directed to Christians because they are commanded to follow Jesus in all things, but you have the opportunity to see what the Bible says about your spiritual situation. I warn you: the language the Bible uses to describe the current state of your heart, mind, and eternal soul is not gentle. Don't be offended. I used to walk where you now are, on that wide comfortable road that leads to destruction. My hope is that you will recognize the Bible's accuracy about your current state and accept Christ's offer for a full life here and eternal life in the future.

Let's get started. In 2 Corinthians 6:14-16, we read, "Do not be yoked together with unbelievers. For what do righteousness and wickedness have in common? Or what fellowship can light have with darkness? What harmony is there between Christ and anti-Christ? What does a believer have in common with an unbeliever? What agreement is there between the temple of God and idols? For we are the temple of the living God." As we have seen, Paul wrote extensively about marriage in his letter to the Corinthian church. Here, he asks five questions that lead his readers to the same obvious conclusion. Each one repeats the idea: "What does this near straight thing have to do with that far-off bent thing?" This is Paul's evidence that a believer should not be consecrated to an unbeliever.

Do you remember what we've said about bentness? Each of us is bent by nature. We have an inner being that has been darkened. We think deep thoughts and hold deep counsels within ourselves, but these judgments are affected negatively by our darkened state. Our spirits sense, feel, and hold conviction, but we enjoy sin, even though it leads us to negative behavior and eternal destruction. Christians have moved into a different space and stand in a different camp. Their bentness is being undone, untwisted, and straightened by their new master. Colossians 1:21-22 describes this move: "Once you were alienated from God and were enemies in your minds because of your evil behavior. But now he has reconciled you by Christ's physical body through death to present you holy in his sight, without blemish and free from accusation."

So, because we have a "spirit" or "soul," we are more than just physical matter. We bear a conscious mind. For Christians, our minds and souls are cleansed and filled by God's Spirit in order to make us clean and to free us from evil. As our spirits are tempted, we are convicted and empowered to resist the bent spiritual influences in the world. As Paul states, "Our struggle is not against flesh and blood, but against the rulers, against the authorities, against the powers of this dark world and against the spiritual forces of evil in the heavenly realms. Therefore put on the full armor of God, so that when the day of evil comes, you may be able to stand your ground, and after you have done everything, to stand" (Ephesians 6:12-13).

We are tempted internally by our cravings and externally by spiritual forces, but we have the armor of God for both defense and offense (truth, righteousness, readiness, faith, salvation, and the Word of God). If we identify ourselves with Christ, He and His teachings influence us. We get our identity, value, and guidelines from Him. God cleanses us through the Holy Spirit and reconciles us to Himself. We stand with His armor and live for Him.

Behind every person is a spiritual attitude, but not every attitude is from the Spirit of God. In 1 Timothy 4:1-2 we read, "God's Spirit clearly says that in later times some will abandon the faith and follow deceiving spirits and things taught by demons. Such teachings come through hypocritical liars, whose consciences have been seared as with a hot iron." There are many people who do not accept Christ because they are "seared" into their bentness. To "sear" a steak is to scorch the surface of it with intense heat so it will retain its juices in subsequent cooking. It crisps the outside and toughens the steak's crust so nothing can pass out or in. The surface becomes less porous and the meat less pliable.

Those who continue to reject Christ show they have had their consciences seared. They become more and more rigid against Him and less and less teachable. If they do not repent, they will inevitably reject the identity, values, and guidelines of Christ. Furthermore, other spiritual influences will begin to influence them. They will get their identity, values, and guidelines from somewhere else—and it's not a good source. They will continue to live solely under the influence of their twisted behavior. They may desire to find life, but left to themselves they will choose decay every time. They are still fully "bent."

Paul simply asks, what do *Christians* have in common with *them*? The answer is nothing. One is near to God; the other is far from Him. One confesses sin as it is revealed in the light; the other hides in the darkness. One is built up in Jesus; the other is torn down by Satan. One believes in the supernatural Jesus; the other rejects Him. One attempts to be worshipful, holy, and pleasing to God; the other worships mortal men and women, money, sex, and power. The two things are water and oil. They cannot mix. They *do not* mix.

Believers	Unbelievers
Righteous	Wicked
Light	Darkness
Christ's possession	Satan's possession
Having belief	Void of belief
Temple of God	Temple of Idols

Life-long partners must depend on each another to uphold the identity, values, and guidelines of the home. As Jesus teaches, "If a kingdom is divided against itself, that kingdom cannot stand. If a house is divided against itself, that house cannot stand" (Mark 3:24-25). John Stott writes, "Neither Christian believing nor Christian loving is to be indiscriminate."[3] In fact, Christian faith is not to be mistaken for gullibility. If we have true faith in Christ, we examine other objects against Him before putting our confidence in them.

Just as doctors are subjected to an examination of their character and competency before the Ontario College of Physicians and Surgeons will accept them and allow them to practice, so we must examine the spirit of a person before we accept him or her and allow that person to partner with us as life-mates. If we find the other person does not share our treasured faith, we must not give our heart to him or her. If that individual doesn't understand the grace of God through Jesus Christ, then he or she isn't God's choice for us.

Imagine sitting on a plane and hearing the flight attendant say, "In case of emergency, put on your own mask, and then help children." Imagine you are married. What if a crisis arose but your spouse sitting next to you refused to put on his mask and held you back from putting on yours? The procedure is simple. You would simply fill your lungs with oxygen and then supply your child with life-giving air. But what if he insisted the oxygen was toxic and wouldn't let you? This is what it's like being married to someone who doesn't share your belief in Christ. Don't do it.

LOUNGING IS FUN, BUT BE CAUTIOUS

When we lounge on the plane, it is really enjoyable. We all look out the window, make conversation, and anticipate the destination. If we are there with someone whom we are interested in, it can be exciting. But for all of the reasons in this chapter, please be cautious. Lounging has its pitfalls and heartbreaks. Lounging can lead to messy spills and agitated passengers. Take care to enjoy the journey with vision and preparedness.

Seven
BAGGAGE CLAIMS

DECLARE YOUR BAGGAGE BEFORE MARRIAGE

Imagine being on your honeymoon and your husband tells you he sold his younger brother into slavery earlier in life. Imagine being on your honeymoon and your wife tells you she used to be married to another man, but he died, and out of poverty she moved into your area. Imagine being in the hospital after the birth of your first child and your husband tells you he was a soldier who had to execute an innocent man. Imagine being married for five years and then finding some old love letters. When you confront your wife, she admits to you that she was involved with another man early on in your relationship. These are not similar cases, but each would drastically change your understanding of your partner.

These are all real-life examples. These kind of things happen. People make regretful decisions. People are put in precarious situations. Life gets messy because of our human bentness. As a result, each of us carries the consequences of past situations and decisions we have made. Each of us carries the memories of old sinful experiences. Some of us may attempt to hide these things from our future spouse. We hope to conceal these things to avoid a ripple effect in the new relationship. We shouldn't do this. Instead of dating with no end in mind, we must be determined to be upfront and honest in our dating relationships. We have to declare our baggage before marriage.

We don't carry baggage alone. When we are weighed down, our partner is also lowed down. It is impossible to exit out of the terminal and rush down the aisle hand-in-hand if one or both are loaded down with unresolved baggage. So, during courtship, we need to be honest about ourselves so our boyfriend or girlfriend really knows us.

Some of us are carrying sexual baggage from previous relationships. Some of us are carrying memories from our childhood, or with our peers, or from other bilateral relations. We could court someone for twelve years without telling that person, if we so decided. But time will not solve this problem. Courage will. We cannot hide these things from our future spouse.

HONESTY AND FORGIVENESS

One of my Australian friends, a pastor in Sydney, just recently said to me, "People need to marry people at their worst." Do you get that? If you accept someone at his or her worst, you have the ability to move upward toward his or her best. You are willing to work at it even though you know everything about that person. However, if you only accept someone at his or her best or middle-good, you will experience shock and disappointment each time that person reveals something below your expectations. You will be disheartened to go down to that person's level, where the work must be done. My friend shared this because he understands the power of forgiveness and the need for true reconciliation in relationships.

We have to be willing to forgive the person in the deepest and darkest situations for us to be vulnerable in the future. This starts before the "I do's." If we can't forgive someone of his or her wrongs, we certainly shouldn't marry that person. If we *can* forgive someone, it is a major step along the path toward consecration. We are able to declare the relationship sacred and holy only after we have done our best to make it pure. Paul shows us what purity looks like: "When we were still powerless, Christ died for the ungodly" (Romans 5:6). John writes, "If we confess our sins, he is faithful and just and will forgive us our sins and purify us from all unrighteousness" (1 John 1:9).

Here again is the example of Jesus for us to follow. He died for us at our worst. He paid for our worst sins. He offers forgiveness to us if we believe in Him, even though we are powerless to undo or repay our debts to God. Forgiveness is to cancel a debt, and Jesus cancels our debt whenever we ask Him through faith and repentance. Furthermore, this redemption purifies us. God declares us holy and pleasing in His sight. The Father in all His power and might and eternral Kingship calls, redeems, and empowers those of us who will turn away from our sins to be clean.

Being honest with your boyfriend, girlfriend, or fiancée releases the floodgates of your past experiences. As each new piece of rubbish flows past, that person has the opportunity to scoop it out of the stream, see it for its ugliness, and discard it by throwing it into a heap. Your fiancée has the ability to purify your part of the relationship—to stand at the altar and declare, "I know this person. I have incinerated his or her past through loving forgiveness, and this person is clean in my sight." Your fiancée will truly regard the relationship with great respect and reverence and commit to being faithful to all of you. As Proverbs 24:26 declares, "An honest answer is like a kiss on the lips."

You can't go around living two different lives or speaking two different sets of lines. It's too much weight on your back. David, the son of Jesse, the slayer of Goliath, knew this weight too well. In Psalm 32:1-5, he wrote:

Blessed is he
> whose transgressions are forgiven,
> whose sins are covered.

Blessed is the man
> whose sin the LORD does not count against him
> and in whose spirit is no deceit.

When I kept silent,
> my bones wasted away
> through my groaning all day long.

For day and night
> your hand was heavy upon me;

my strength was sapped
> as in the heat of summer.

Then I acknowledged my sin to you
> and did not cover up my iniquity.

I said, "I will confess
> my transgressions to the LORD"—

and you forgave
> the guilt of my sin.

This personal journal from David, in the form of a psalm, describes the experience of the sinner who finds forgiveness from the Lord. At first he avoids God. He feels as though he is wasting away. He feels drained. He groans because of the burden of his deception. Finally, after enduring this ongoing pain for months and months, he reveals his sin to God. Of course, God already knew it, but He is now able to receive the confession because the man's heart is truly broken and apologetic. When the confession happens, he feels free, released, and alive!

People often say "you have to forgive yourself" or "you have to forgive that other person," but they don't often mention this first part about finding forgiveness from God. We must always go to the Lord first for His forgiveness, because only after we have received forgiveness will we understand how to forgive. Once we have admitted our sin to God and He has removed his heavy hand from our back, we can duplicate a similar type of freedom within our human relationships. We will know how to ask for it and how to give it.

As one person openly asks for forgiveness and the other openly gives it, the feelings of wasting away, the sensation of draining heat, and the silence are removed because the guilt is removed. In Matthew 6:12, Jesus shows us an example of this in prayer: "Forgive us our debts, as we also have forgiven our debtors." Paul gives us this command in life: "Be kind and compassionate to one another, forgiving each other, just as in Christ God forgave you" (Ephesians 4:32).

The more we hold things in, or fail to release them, or refuse to be honest about them, or conceal the latches so God and the other person can't see into our hearts, the more rubbish we will accumulate. The weight will build until eventually we will be crushed. For example, many couples find it difficult to initiate sexual conversations and openly discuss individual needs and desires because much of the issue is rooted in the unknowns of history. A wife may be surprised because her husband gets defensive if she openly makes some small suggestions, but his defensiveness may arise because he questions where the suggestions are coming from. A husband may be frustrated because his wife constantly turns down his plans to try new things or incorporate new rituals into their love play, but her resistance may arise because she wonders from where those things in left field originated.

You can have forgiveness from God if you ask Him and own up to all of your sin by confessing it specifically. You can also have forgiveness from your fiancée if you confess your sin to him or her specifically. When confession and forgiveness occur, you will both feel clean, free, released, and alive! You may need someone from the outside to ask honest hard-hitting questions through a process that has been thoughtfully prayed about and set out. Have you met with a Bible-believing pastor yet? If not, you really should. Pre-marital counseling will help unearth these things in a caring and intentional environment.

Also know that forgiveness is a process. In Matthew 18:21, Peter asked Jesus, "Lord, how many times shall I forgive my brother when he sins against me? Up to seven times?" Jesus answered, "I tell you, not seven times, but seventy times seven" (verse 22). As you read Jesus' words, you might naturally think of forgiving the same person for 490 different offences. The need for this is entirely possible, as those who live in close proximity to each other will hurt one another hundreds of times. But what about forgiving the same person 490 different times for just one offense? Murray Vassar, a student at Asbury Theological Seminary, puts it this way:

> I realize now that forgiveness is rarely a one-time event. Jesus calls us to forgive. A few hours later, when the memories return, he calls us to forgive again. When we wake up the next morning, and the memories are still there, he calls us to forgive again. Six months later, when we have long passed 490, he calls us to forgive again. The forgiveness Jesus calls us to offer is more of a habit or a disposition than a discrete act.[1]

Because sex is within you, the personal memories and offenses can easily resurface. You will have to start your marriage with the disposition of forgiveness and continue to practice forgiveness throughout your life. But if you don't start there, it will be much harder to learn later on. One young husband I know texted these words to his wife:

I totally forgive you for the sins of your past, right up until yesterday. I have no claim over you. You don't owe me anything. We journey together by grace. I declare this to you now and will strive to live it out. I will not make references to your past anymore. I trust you to respond to me as God leads you. Thank you for forgiving my sins. I truly am sorry for them and I seek to be purer man. I am sorry for being insecure when I don't understand you. I am glad we talked.

DO THE NARNIAN HORSES ROLL?

C.S. Lewis wrote one of my favorite books, *The Horse and His Boy*. My father read this book to me as a child, and I have read this material to both of my sons. It is a story about a journey, about an adventure, and about becoming a honorable man. It is also a story of redemption, for a young boy journeys from rejection and slavery into a new land of acceptance and kingship.

Shasta, the main character, grows up in a small fishing village where he is cared for and yet oppressed by his adoptive father. There at the sea, he keeps dreaming of the North. One day an important guest arrives, and Shasta is left to care for the stranger's horse. During this encounter, the horse reveals he is a talking horse from the land of Narnia. He tells Shasta how he was caught as a young foal and has been away from home all his life.

During the course of the evening, the horse recruits the boy to journey across the country of Calormine and over the desert to return to Narnia and the North. The two go through many adventures. As Shasta learns how to ride and how to have courage, we learn that Bree, the horse, is much more intelligent than any of the dumb horses of Calormine, who do not speak. He talks like a human. He reasons as a human.

Along the way, Bree begins to fret about his poor upbringing. Over time we find that he is worried about the habits he may have picked up from being among the dumb horses in the country of his captivity. He constantly asks, "Do Narnian horses roll?" The dumb horses of Calormine *do* role, and Bree finds great pleasure in this habit. But now, as he gets closer to his own country of Narnia, he is unsure if this behavior is appropriate for horses of greater nobility.

Many of us live like Bree before we enter marriage. We've had previous experiences or thoughts. We've had certain conversations, or kisses, or touches. Moreover, we may have seen things on television and the Internet. Many of these sights and smells are full sensual pleasure, and we secretly hope we will live them out in our married relationship. Yet we wonder if these expectations are appropriate for a noble husband and noble wife. We know we've been tainted by the dumb culture around us. We know we've picked up bad habits and seen things that are impure. Now we are unsure if we will have to give up some of those behaviors or if we will be able to hold on to them. Which pleasures are sinful? Which joys of sex are pure?

When Bree meets other talking horses, he is confronted with something that is certainly inappropriate: his pride. As he grew up among the dumb horses, he picked up the habit of thinking he was overly intelligent. He is rebuked quite harshly for this. It seems that Bree is a common talking horse. In the same way, as we enter marriage, there are many things—such as viewing pornography, pressuring our spouse to do things that are knowingly uncomfortable, committing adultery, and other personal twisted behaviors—that are clearly inappropriate to give and receive pure sexual love. We must be rebuked of these things. These are habits we must renounce, and we must set strict boundaries against them.

However, as Bree comes to realize, Narnian horses do indeed roll! Christian men and women do enjoy great sex. There are many things that noble people do sexually. Sex is in no way dirty if the marriage bed is kept pure. It is the ultimate form of body language. It is an amazing tool. It is one of the crafts of love-speaking. It is a gift from the very hand of God to give us blissful joy. So how do you choose between the bad habits of our culture, some of which you must release, and the effective touches and massages of a noble and pleasure giving/receiving lover? What do you do to reset your expectations to enable a pure and powerful connection with your spouse?

Gratitude and Love

Imagine a picture of a nerdy person holding the hand of a really beautiful person. They are gazing into each other's eyes. Underneath, the caption reads, "Thank you." One who is naturally beautiful might think the nerd is saying thanks. One who is naturally intelligent might think the beauty is saying thanks. In reality, both are saying thanks because they appreciate the other for their own uniqueness.

It is rare to find someone who is completely comfortable in his or her own skin and temperament. We all have our faults and our deficiencies. Most of these things have less to do with our bodies than with our actions and attitudes. We know that we cannot live up to the professor-like intelligence, politician-like communication, martial-art-like physicality, and heroic-like selflessness we see portrayed in every hero and heroine of fiction. We do struggle to have a good body image, because models are airbrushed and actors are on elite diets.

This is where love and gratitude enable us to overcome our own insecurities. In 1 Corinthians 13:4-7, Paul says, "Love is patient, love is kind. It does not envy, it does not boast, it is not proud. It is not rude, it is not self-seeking, it is not easily angered, it keeps no record of wrongs. Love does not delight in evil but rejoices with the truth. It always protects, always trusts, always hopes, always perseveres." This is perfect love. We can have self-acceptance, self-esteem, and a good body image not because of our own perfection but because of our partner's faithful love, which involves consideration and enduring commitment.

I am thankful for my wife's love because I'm such a wretch at heart. I struggle with bitter envy and selfish ambition. I don't treat her with a wholesome, perfect-patient love that God intends for me. I can't be that guy on the magazine cover. I can't be that hulk. But my perfection is not really the point of our marriage, is it? The point is that she loves me despite the fact that I am not all of these things. She stood up one day and declared herself to me for better or worse. She gave me a gift, and it is a gift I have received with gratitude. Her devotion to me is like gold in a treasure chest.

When we understand our spouse loves us, and our gratitude works to bring us into a humble and peaceful state of mind, we can then focus on arousing our mate and experience the joyful personal pleasure of sex. Dr. Douglas Rosenau writes, "Think of how difficult it is to sexually focus on your mate when you are embarrassed, inhibited, or self-conscious.... 'Sexy' in a God-given sense is a state of mind and not the shape of our bodies or our weight. If you learn to accept your body and revel in your sexual feelings, your mate will follow suit and be tremendously turned on by you."[2]

Veggie Tales has a fun song that says the same thing: "Because a thankful heart is a happy heart! I'm glad for what I have, that's an easy way to start!"

Openness and Attentiveness

There is a whole realm of issues we have to consider for good lovemaking. Each of us has hopes and expectations, likes and dislikes, and different on/off switches. Topics such as positions, sights, smells in the bedroom, dances outside the bedroom, food, and certain types of touching or kissing are up for debate as you default yourself to be your partner's love.

You may have enjoyed some things in past relationships and hope to enjoy them in your marriage relationship. You may have regretted certain things and plan to avoid them. The association of old memories plays a significant role in fashioning what you want. This is not good, but it is a reality for many people. The best-case scenario is two newly married virgins finding out their likes and dislikes together, but we have already covered the need to be honest with each other and the need to forgive each others' past sin, because the problem is common.

It is time to be open and attentive to the pleasures of our spouse. Our lovemaking can't be full of dishonesty and inattentiveness to each other. We must focus the conversations about lovemaking on the needs and desires of both people. We must be open and attentive to the other person even if it draws out old wounds. How do we overcome the past? How do we decide on which things to include in order to move forward? The short answer is a question that we must answer as a married couple: *what is comfortable for us both?*

Openness and attentiveness sometimes pull at each other. "I don't like that, but he does. I like it when she does that to me, but she doesn't." Openness is being truthful with the other person so our needs are met. We state what brings us joy and what are our hopes. Attentiveness is being loving enough so that the other person's needs are met. We listen gently and patiently to what brings our spouse joy and what are his or her hopes. Great sex happens when both of these worlds literally collide. As two bodies join to become one, the process of open and attentive collision creates the ultimate climax and orgasm.

I have found the book *A Celebration of Sex* by Dr. Douglas Rosenau to be very helpful. He writes, "Great sex is based on mature lovers who can be honest with themselves and their mates. They are self-aware and can assertively communicate."[3] In Ephesians 4:15, Paul explains, "Speaking the truth in love, we will *in all things grow up*." Our lovemaking will "grow up" as we communicate with openness (truth) and attentiveness (love). Listen to this kind of talk between a husband and wife in Song of Solomon 4:15–16:

> HUSBAND, THE TENOR SINGER:
> You are a garden fountain,
> > a well of flowing water streaming down.
>
> WIFE, THE SOPRANO SINGER:
> Awake, north wind,
> > and come, south wind!
> Blow on my garden,
> > that its fragrance may spread abroad.

Do you see how the husband describes his wife? Do you see how she instructs him to come to her? This kind of back-and-forth wordplay can be helpful to us in our relationships. It is being truthful and open to say, "I'm attracted to your body and stimulated by it." It is loving attentiveness to then say, "Come, let's blow on each other."

CREATIVITY AND ROMANCE

Sex is not as straightforward as it looks. It is not perfect, and it changes over time. As bodies and families change, so do our sexual desires and needs. As they say, variety is the spice of life. Creativity and romance act as the hallway to the spice drawer.

In order to add something new into the relationship, we must understand this principle. Great sex does not come by having lots of experience with many partners but by working to create romance with one life-long partner. Think about this this way: Once we've purchased the ingredients for our meal, we're secure about it and get to make adjustments as we need, just for the pleasure of it. One night we might add fast heat; on another occasion we might go with a longer simmer. We can work at our cooking skills for as long as we are able—in some cases, until death parts us. This is a fantastic way to get the chemistry of the meal perfect.

We have the rest of our lives to taste and touch, figure out what we like and don't like, and work together to perfect things by thinking outside the norm and creating romantic gestures. We can use thoughtful gifts, sensual movements (dances or massages), different lighting, sweet smells, and descriptive words in a safe and secure environment to bring creativity and romance into the bedroom. The meal goes on and on, and we get to make it better and better.

Anticipation and Responsiveness

In music, anticipation occurs when part of a chord is played that is about to resolve in full. When we hear it, we arrange in our minds what will soon come to completion in the full expression of the chord. In lovemaking, anticipation is the arrangement of thoughtful details in advance of the act that is about to follow in timely succession. Anticipation begins in our mind, but it doesn't just remain an exercise of fantasy. We think about our lover and fantasize about some experience to think about things to do, but then we arrange for something specific to happen to ensure a full, complete, and climatic experience.

Responsiveness is saying yes to the preparation we see our spouse laying out for us. It is walking through the door that has just been opened. We don't shut our spouse down, and we don't stop the anticipation. We join his or her fantasy planning and help our spouse bring it to full expression. For example, when a wife arrives home from a flight, she could anticipate her husband's longing to be kissed. So she will make sure she gives her husband a long embrace and touches him lip to lip right when they step into the arrivals terminal. He will welcome it.

The husband might then anticipate his wife's desire to be pampered, so he will make sure he is first to the door so he can open it for her. She will let him. He might arrange to have a map with directions so they can stop at a restaurant for a glass of wine. She will say yes to the catch-up on conversation. She might dress in a certain way and select some music for later. When they get home, he will joyfully and quickly bring her to the bedroom.

WIFE, THE SOPRANO SINGER:
Let him kiss me with the kisses of his mouth—
    for your love is more delightful than wine
    (Song of Solomon 1:2).

PLANNING AND DISCIPLINE

One tool we can use to protect oneness is "marriage time."[4] These are planned out times we set aside to reconnect with our spouse. Both partners must be disciplined to ensure its reoccurrence. Note that these times should be:

- Planned: We need to put it in our calendar. Make it a task to be completed. Prioritize this time above other things so it doesn't get bumped too often.
- Protected: We need to reserve this time with our spouse. Do this by saying things like, "I already have an appointment that night," or "I can't do that event because the time is already blocked off in my calendar," or "I can't complete that assignment by tomorrow morning, because I have plans tonight with my spouse. Can I complete it by noon tomorrow?"
- Thoughtful: If we want to land in the "sweet spot" so our spouse smiles and feels special, we have to put in the effort and pay attention to the things he or she likes to do. I've been married for sixteen years now, and I know that I have to think outside my box in order to be anywhere near her box.
- Mutual: It is best to take turns planning this protected time with our spouse. This way, both parties feel the intentional love of the other person.

Too many people put their careers and recreational activities before their spouse. One young woman said to me, "A truly worthy spouse would be understanding of my professional aspirations." This is backward, because if you plan, protect, and create thoughtful and mutually shared marriage time, you will make yourself a worthy spouse who understands the real value of your marriage.

Eight
ARRIVAL

THE WEDDING DAY

Imagine watching your beloved arrive on your wedding day. Perhaps, men, she has just walked through the doors, or out into the garden, or into your church. Perhaps, women, he is standing at the front while everyone is looking at you. You both are trying to get a glimpse of the one you love. You both anticipate his or her hand on your arm. You both anticipate the mouth-to-mouth kiss...

You both say I do. You kiss and embrace. You anticipate the evening with family and friends, followed by a night of passionate sex. You've arrived. You are married!

Perhaps it wasn't an easy arrival. Sometimes, the world of the engaged is directly in between being-a-child-to-my-parent and being-a-partner-to-my-fiancée. Maybe you saw this when multiple parties got involved planning your wedding. Often, parents have their own views about what should happen and how it should look. For example, they often feel that if guests have traveled a great distance, they are due an expensive and refined meal. It is normal for the engaged couple to come into conflict with competing opinions about the actual day.

Maybe your family has some traditions you can include with minimal interference to show your respect. I encourage you to honor your family as much as you can. Even though this requires patience and accommodation, work out the details so your family feels esteemed.

That being said, maybe your family's ideas might be too extreme to be considered. You need to stand your ground regarding things of a moral nature and spiritual conviction. Set your plans as an independent, mature couple in these matters, and include only enough space for others' requests if they are neutral (e.g., letting a brother give the speech to the bride, cutting the cake at 8:00 p.m. rather than 7:30 p.m., or having Aunt May do the flowers).

Now that the day is on its way, I encourage you to choose vows that include references to Christ. I also encourage you to incorporate worship and meaningful reflections from God's Word throughout the day. Furthermore, make sure God is a part of the ceremony *and* the reception. Many a wedding has gone by the wayside after a couple stood before God in the church only to be a part of a drunken bash at the back of the hall.

The Bible records many happy occasions, even weddings, where alcohol was present. But you should never intend for your guests to get drunk. I encourage all my wedding couples to avoid an open bar or a cash bar, because these types of arrangements often diminish God's glory as people start to lose self-control.

LIVING PICTURES WITHIN YOUR HOME

You've heard the phrase, "A picture is worth a thousand words." Still pictures have the power to make an impact. When we see something in all its fullness and brightness, we appreciate its beauty. Movies are moving pictures. At thirty frames per second, a two-hour film is worth 216,000 stills. When we see the brightness and fullness of an object operating within its larger context, we see how intricate beauty upon beauty becomes. We feel a sense of our smallness and are in awe of God's greatness.

Stills and movies fill our minds with powerful visual stimulation and make an impact. If we watch beautiful goodness, we are lifted. If we watch oppressive darkness, we are pushed down. So I ask you, what could be more powerful than still pictures or moving pictures? The only things more powerful than these are *living pictures*.

This is why having a joyful and faithful marriage relationship is so important to the individual and also to the greater family of God. Not only has God made a long-lasting marriage one of the most powerful, unique, and special opportunities one individual can participate in to help another person feel more secure and significant, but He has also designed the marriage relationship to be a living and breathing picture of His grace. A Christian marriage portrays the love-filled relationship that exists between Christ and the church.

God, knowing the power of living pictures, gives outsiders an opportunity to see the gospel in living color by watching a Christian marriage. Voddie Baucham, pastor of Grace Family Baptist Church, once preached, "It is not because marriage is important in and of itself, even though marriage is important in and of itself, it is because of the gospel."[1] A marriage is a vivid picture of the gospel when it is full of mutual love and commitment along with Christ-like sacrifice and church-like submission.

In Ephesians 5:31–32, Paul states, "A man will leave his father and mother and be united to his wife, and the two will become one flesh. This is a profound mystery, but I am talking about Christ and the church." Thus, as a man sacrifices himself for his wife, he demonstrates Christ's love for the church. As a woman serves her husband, she demonstrates the church's love for Christ. A Christian marriage is one of the signs at the airport that says, "Welcome; look how we bring life to each other and glory to God."

To understand Paul's idea in Ephesians 5, we must first understand how the book of Ephesians exhorts the church to bring glory to Christ.[2] Like many of Paul's writings, this letter has a section of "what God has done" followed by a section of "what we must do." Paul explains what Christ has done on the cross on our behalf and then discusses how we are called, empowered, and motivated to bring glory to Him.

In some of Paul's letters, such as Romans, the division between the theological and practical is clear-cut. In Ephesians, however, Paul uses a general formula seven times to make his point. In the beginning of the letter, his formula emphasizes what God has done. Near the end, the repetition emphasizes what we must do. Each time, the formula repeats the same elements: (1) what we were before we met Christ; (2) what we now are because of Him; (3) how this should lead us to glorify Christ and build up the church. Here are some examples:

EPHESIANS 1:7–9,12, 22–23
In him we have redemption through his blood, the forgiveness of our trespasses, according to the riches of his grace which he lavished

upon us, in all wisdom and insight making known to us the mystery of his will, according to his purpose...so that we who were the first to hope in Christ might be to the praise of his glory.... God placed all things under his feet and appointed him to be head over everything for the church, which is his body, the fullness of him who fills everything in every way.

Ephesians 2:1–2,4–5,12–13
As for you, you were dead in the trespasses and sins in which you once walked, following the course of this world, following the prince of the power of the air, the spirit that is now at work in the sons of disobedience....

But God, being rich in mercy, because of the great love with which he loved us, even when we were dead in our trespasses, made us alive together with Christ—by grace you have been saved....

Therefore remember that you were at that time separated from Christ, alienated from the commonwealth of Israel and strangers to the covenants of promise, having no hope and without God in the world. But now in Christ Jesus you who once were far away have been brought near through the blood of Christ.

Ephesians 2:17–22
He came and preached peace to you who were far away and peace to those who were near. For through him we both have access to the Father by one Spirit. Consequently, you are no longer foreigners and aliens, but fellow citizens with God's people and members of God's household, built on the foundation of the apostles and prophets, with Christ Jesus himself as the chief cornerstone. In him the whole building is joined together and rises to become a holy temple in the Lord. And in him you too are being built together to become a dwelling in which God lives by his Spirit.

Ephesians 4:22–27; 5:1–3, 6–7,15–18; 6:13; 4:16
You were taught, with regard to your former way of life, to put off

your old self, which is being corrupted by its deceitful desires; to be made new in the attitude of your minds; and to put on the new self, created to be like God in true righteousness and holiness. Therefore each of you must put off falsehood and speak truthfully to his neighbor, for we are all members of one body. "In your anger do not sin": Do not let the sun go down while you are still angry, and do not give the devil a foothold....

Be imitators of God, therefore, as dearly loved children and live a life of love, just as Christ loved us and gave himself up for us as a fragrant offering and sacrifice to God. But among you there must not be even a hint of sexual immorality, or of any kind of impurity, or of greed, because these are improper for God's holy people....

Let no one deceive you with empty words, for because of such things God's wrath comes on those who are disobedient. Therefore do not be partners with them....

Be very careful, then, how you live—not as unwise but as wise, making the most of every opportunity, because the days are evil. Therefore do not be foolish, but understand what the Lord's will is. Do not get drunk on wine, which leads to debauchery. Instead, be filled with the Spirit...

Therefore put on the full armor of God, so that when the day of evil comes, you may be able to stand your ground, and after you have done everything, to stand....

[4:16] From him the whole body, joined and held together by every supporting ligament, grows and builds itself up in love, as each part does its work.

Did you notice how in each passage Paul writes more about God's provision at the beginning and then moves to more of our responsibilities at the end? When we get to Ephesians 5:22, we are clearly planted in the "therefore, do these things" section of the book. Applying these verses on marriage reflect the ongoing command for us to glorify God, glorify Christ, and build up the church.

Paul is teaching us to build up the church through Christ. The two central figures of this book are Christ and His church. The gospel is the good news that Christ is being unified with His people because of His sacrifice and their submission. The gospel explains how Christ pours Himself out for His church in humility and how the church glorifies Him through following Him. Paul teaches that the mutual submission of marriage—husband as sacrificial lamb, wife as redeemed following church—becomes a living picture of the gospel.

Ephesians 5:22–32

Wives, submit to your husbands as to the Lord. For the husband is the head of the wife as Christ is the head of the church, his body, of which he is the Savior. Now as the church submits to Christ, so also wives should submit to their husbands in everything. *Husbands,* love your wives, just as Christ loved the church and gave himself up for her to make her holy, cleansing her by the washing with water through the word, and to present her to himself as a radiant church, without stain or wrinkle or any other blemish, but holy and blameless. In this same way, husbands ought to love their wives as their own bodies. He who loves his wife loves himself. After all, no one ever hated his own body, but he feeds and cares for it, just as Christ does the church—for we are members of his body. "For this reason a man will leave his father and mother and be united to his wife, and the two will become one flesh." This is a profound mystery—but I am talking about Christ and the church.

Children are desperate to see the sacrificial love of Christ in their fathers and the submission of the church in their mothers. Neighbors are desperate to see the humility of Christ in men and the purity of the church in women. Everyone needs to see that we are God's workmanship through Christ. For better or worse, our marriage is a living picture in smell, sight, sound, taste, and touch. As we let God transform us, He paints and sculpts us into a powerful picture of the love between Christ and His church. We are the sculptures and fountains that adorn the vast main hall of the arrivals terminal. We say, "Look at us, see Christ, and love the church."

What happens when young people look at our lives and say, "But Christ said you should do this as a woman—what are *you* doing?" What happens when neighbors watch us and say, "I don't understand Jesus when I look at the way you act as a husband—what are you doing?" When we don't live out our scriptural callings as husbands and wives, we become an anti-Christian picture of hypocrisy. We speak against Christ and His church because we refuse to portray an accurate reflection of the gospel. Our young people learn to be hypocrites under our tutelage, and other adults reject the church as being harsh, prideful, and arrogant.

One commentator said it this way: "It is relatively easy to exhibit a Spirit-filled life for one or two hours a week in church, but it takes the work of the Holy Spirit to exhibit godliness not only on Sundays but also in everyday relationships between wives and husbands."[3] Do you see how vitally important it is for us to get this right? God has done the work for us. Now we must live out these things as husbands and wives to bring Him glory and build up His church.

WIVES, SUBMIT TO YOUR HUSBANDS

Notice that Paul writes in Ephesians 5:22–24, "Wives, submit to your husbands as to the Lord. For the husband is the head of the wife as Christ is the head of the church, his body, of which He is the Savior. Now as the church submits to Christ, so also wives should submit to their husbands in everything."

Paul's statement "as to the Lord" does not mean a wife is to submit to her husband in the same way she submits to the Lord. Rather, her submission to her husband is a service rendered "to the Lord." To bring clarity to this, in Colossians 3:23 we read, " Whatever you do, work at it with all your heart, as working for the Lord, not for men." Ladies, when you submit to your husband with sincerity of heart and reverence for Christ, it is an act of service to Christ. You worship Christ when you respect the leadership and headship of your husband.

The Power of Submission

You might wonder when Paul says "the husband is the head of the wife as Christ is the head of the church" why marriage should not be an equal partnership. God has created the relationship to reflect the headship in the church. In the same way He appointed Christ to lead the church, he has appointed husbands to lead their wives. If we believe that God is good, we will trust that this design in marriage is also good.

Now, a guy might respond to this by saying, "That's right. Did you here that, sister? I am the *head*, like Jesus our Savior." If you know someone like this, you might think, *That can't be right. I know this man, and he can barely spell Jesus, let alone be like Him*. This verse could draw out pride in men, but it should actually stir up sobriety and responsibility in them. God has given men responsibility for the physical and spiritual wellbeing of their wives and children.

On the other hand, this verse could cause fear in women. "What if I give him control?" they might ask. "What will he do with it? What if I give him respect and honor? Will he step all over me?" Skepticism shouldn't be our response either. Just as God set out the most beautiful plan of salvation for all people in Christ, He is the same all-knowing, all-powerful, all-present God who has designed women to reflect the submission of the church in marriage.

Take a minute to let that sink in. God has specifically designed women to be a beautiful and powerful reflection of Christ's bride—pure, spotless, gentle, respectful, powerful, forceful, glorious, and triumphant. All of these characteristics can be found within submission. Each of these words describes the church as she submits to Christ. It will work in a wife's favor to look like the church in her marriage.

Christ's Agent

Paul concludes by saying, "Now as the church submits to Christ, so also wives should submit to their husbands in everything." This makes it clear the wife is not submitting because the husband is superior. It really doesn't matter if he's a rock star or just a rock. She submits to Him because she works for Christ. She is Christ's agent, working for the Lord and not for men, gifted and uniquely skilled to be a living picture of the church's submission to Christ.

The wife shows her husband what the church should be like. She shows him the power of the church working in daily life. She helps him see the benefit of staying with the church family as she invites him to work through conflict and lead in decision-making. As she and her husband overcome difficulty and experience joy, she helps him be faithful to the church and demonstrates what patient faithfulness looks like. She shows how Christ transforms those who submit to Him by submitting to her husband. Peter writes a parallel command:

> Wives, in the same way be submissive to your husbands so that, if any of them do not believe the word, they may be won over without words by the behavior of their wives, when they see the purity and reverence of your lives. Your beauty should not come from outward adornment, such as braided hair and the wearing of gold jewelry and fine clothes. Instead, it should be that of your inner self, the unfading beauty of a gentle and quiet spirit, which is of great worth in God's sight. For this is the way the holy women of the past who put their hope in God used to make themselves beautiful. They were submissive to their own husbands, like Sarah, who obeyed Abraham and called him her master. You are her daughters if you do what is right and do not give way to fear (1 Peter 3:1–6).

Men struggle to believe that kindness and gentleness are ways to resolve conflict. They struggle to believe in the power of the church, because they see conflict and pain. Men also struggle with selfishness. Their sinful nature is to battle, fight, debate, argue, and hoard. Women are agents of Christ to preach against these things as they embody gentleness and purity. Proverbs 16:32 says, "Better a patient man than a warrior, a man who controls his temper than one who takes a city." We naturally look at that and say, "Yeah, right. Tell that to Alexander the Great." However, God's Word is true, and women can convince men of it by bringing glory to Christ and building up the church when they submit to their husbands.

Women, do you want a real adventure? Do you want your life to count for a glorious cause? Do you hope that your day-to-day actions will add up to something greater than the sum total of your days? Then be an agent of Christ to your husband. You have a unique opportunity to preach the church to your husband.

One Specific Application for Wives

As we've discussed, sex is generally more important to men. So, wives, have a responsive attitude to your husband's sexual advances and make him feel desired. Have a ministry of sexual intimacy to your husband. Take pleasure in giving him pleasure. As Paul writes:

> The husband should fulfill his marital duty to his wife, and likewise the wife to her husband. The wife's body does not belong to her alone but also to her husband. In the same way, the husband's body does not belong to him alone but also to his wife. Do not deprive each other except by mutual consent and for a time, so that you may devote yourselves to prayer. Then come together again so that Satan will not tempt you because of your lack of self-control (1 Corinthians 7:3–5).

In this passage, Paul instructs married couples about how to avoid sexual temptation outside the marriage bed: "Do not deprive each other except by mutual consent." Problems arise when one partner deprives the other. When this occurs, the marginalized party is tempted to find significance elsewhere because of his or her lack of self-control. Both parties contribute to the problem, and both parties contribute to the solution.

As Paul notes, both parties are to serve one another's intimate needs. His solution is for husbands and wives to come together as often as is mutually needed. The husband fulfills what the wife needs, which could be intercourse, because she is aroused. Or it might mean intercourse to fulfill her desire to have a baby. Or she may just want a nice massage or a cuddle. It might include a date night away from the kids or a conversation about upcoming events. Whatever form it takes, the husband pays attention to the intimate needs of his wife concerning friendship and sex.

At the same time, the wife fulfills what her husband needs—which will be much more sexual in nature. This could be intercourse to nourish his sexual appetite, or sexual touching so that he climaxes. He may want a massage after a hard day and end it with tender lovemaking. He may have had an emotional day at work and needs to talk things out or to be consoled by his wife's body. Sex is a powerful communication tool. A married man thrives when his wife communicates her love to him by being sexual with him. A married man can run into real problems when there is a lack in the quality and quantity of sex.

This is what Solomon's wife says about their lovemaking:

> Like an apple tree among the trees of the forest
> > is my lover among the young men.
> I delight to sit in his shade,
> > and his fruit is sweet to my taste.
> He has taken me to the banquet hall,
> > and his banner over me is love.
> Strengthen me with raisins,
> > refresh me with apples,
> > for I am faint with love.
> His left arm is under my head,
> > and his right arm embraces me (Song of Solomon 2:3–6).

Here is a woman who takes joy in the lovemaking process because she recognizes the value of her husband. She speaks of her lover as a strong apple tree. She delights in being under him and tasting him, for he has taken her into his home and loved her. She now responds by calling for him to put his left arm under her head and his right arm under her naked body.

Wives, if your husband feels he isn't getting enough sex or that you don't desire him, he will translate it into a form of rejection. He will be hurt and will feel anger. However, if you can anticipate sex and plan out how to utilize this tool of lovemaking to show him your appreciation, you will help him remain strong and alive. Mark Gungor has a humorous way to say it:

"The way to her happy place is through her heart. The way to his heart is through his happy place."[4]

As the husband lays himself down for his beloved bride, his sexual attraction for her grows. As he spends time listening and being with her, he wants to be physically intimate as well. As he cuddles, he hopes the cuddling will "have a purpose." Therefore, be joyfully responsive to his subtle advances for affection. You can make him feel important without going all the way to sex by simply saying, "Yes, come kiss me. I love you too." You can inject love into his veins by simply touching him, hugging him, and telling him what you plan to do to him at a later time. The idea that it is okay for him to love you physically throughout the day will be very powerful for him.

Moreover, be joyfully responsive to his advances for sex. If you use sex to manipulate your husband, or if you withhold your physical love from him, or if your sexuality comes across as duty, you are making him feel insignificant. Canadian singer, songwriter, and story teller Steve Bell wrote a song in which the chorus said, "Can we be all alone tonight, just to be what we both know is right?" He wrote it sitting on a bus as he was going home from a gig. He was longing for his wife to be planning intimacy.[5]

Every guy identifies with this. They long to be refreshed by the smile, the words, and the body of their wife. Can you say that you love to be under his tree? Will you make it a priority to plan for sexual intimacy and say, "Refresh me with raisins and apples for I am faint with love"? The power of the climax "yes" in the midst of passionate lovemaking is simply ecstasy.

For those who are married with kids, this requires dedication and commitment to see it come to completion. You are often tired and depleted. Sometimes your husband gets home and the kids are still awake or the relatives are still over. Marriage is a blend of romantic grapes mixed with spice-notes of disaster and aged well in the barrels of commitment. It is not about instant gratification but ongoing determination to keep on ministering to one another. Marriage is often like watching something die and be resurrected. It is a journey of tragedy, hardship, tears, inconvenience, headaches, back aches, and "winter trees," so to speak.

Have a ministry of sexual intimacy to your husband. Take pleasure in giving him pleasure. If you do, you will tell him that he is significant to you. The cold times will recede to warmth. The sap will start to flow, buds will turn into flowers, flowers will turn into fruit, and, if you continue to minister, the joy and satisfaction of a friendship combined with continued physical intimacy will strengthen your relationship.

HUSBANDS, LOVE YOUR WIVES

Paul provides these instructions for husbands in Ephesians 5:25-30: "Husbands, love your wives, just as Christ loved the church and gave himself up for her to make her holy, cleansing her by the washing with water through the word, and to present her to himself as a radiant church, without stain or wrinkle or any other blemish, but holy and blameless. In this same way, husbands ought to love their wives as their own bodies. He who loves his wife loves himself. After all, no one ever hated his own body, but he feeds and cares for it, just as Christ does the church—for we are members of his body."

Notice Paul commands husbands to *love* their wives. In 1 John 4:10–12, we find what this means: "This is love: not that we loved God, but that he loved us and sent his Son as an atoning sacrifice for our sins. Dear friends, since God so loved us, we also ought to love one another. No one has ever seen God; but if we love one another, God lives in us and his love is made complete in us." Husbands, your love for your wives is to be a "leader love." Leaders don't wait for others to act first; they act first. When you love your wife, it is a service to Christ because you sacrifice as He sacrificed. Christ, the head of the church, our Savior and leader, knows the power of love expressed through sacrifice.

PREACHING THE CROSS THROUGH LOVE

Paul states that husbands are to love their wives "just as Christ loved the church and gave himself up for her, cleansing her through the word." There are three ways husbands are to be like Christ toward their wives: (1) by deciding to be the first to act for her benefit, (2) by giving himself up for her, and (3) by cleansing her through the Word of God.

Now, a woman might respond to this by saying, "Did you hear that, boy? You are supposed to give me whatever I want. A happy wife is a happy life." If you know a someone like that, you might think, *That can't be right. She's spoiled. She just wants me to listen and give in to her every wish.* This verse could stir up some stubbornness or resentfulness in men, but it shouldn't. The purpose of a man's love is to transform his wife through God's power working through him. He depends on the work of Christ to work in her rather than oppressing her.

Peter writes a parallel command: "Husbands, in the same way be considerate as you live with your wives, and treat them with respect as the weaker partner and as heirs with you of the gracious gift of life, so that nothing will hinder your prayers" (1 Peter 3:7). Even though husbands could rule over their wives physically, they instead show their wives what the love of Christ is as they pour themselves out for them. Why? Because they are co-heirs and highly valued. The husband preaches the cross—that someone would lay down his life for an imperfect sinner. He shows his wife Christ's love by the way he loves. He shows her the beauty of her Savior by drawing her to His story and directing her to the teachings of Christ.

Women have the sinful tendency to want control in the church, in the home, and in relationships. They utilize all their relational attunement to sway things to their advantage. Women also struggle to leave well enough alone and try to take over God's work. As Proverbs 21:19 states, it is "better to live in a desert than with a quarrelsome and ill-tempered wife." However, a husband can convince his wife of Christ's ways by bringing glory to Him and building up the church through his sacrifice for her. He can preach amazing sermons of sacrificial love to his wife simply by sacrificing his desires for her and directing her eyes to Scripture.

BLESSING THROUGH SACRIFICE

Husbands, you might be afraid of doing what she wants. You might say, "What if I don't like it? What if she sees it as weakness? Will she start trying to lead?" God says that she is your body. As you love her, you love yourself. Both you and your wife will experience an intrinsic increase in blessing as you sacrifice for her. Here is a short list of ways to do this:

Act First
- Give up your wants to fulfill her needs.
- Pick up the kids and play with them.
- Help around the house even when you're tired.
- Stay at home from sports for a time.
- Listen to her voice.
- Esteem her and acknowledge her advice about your life, your work, your relationships, and your church family.

Go to the Word with Her
- Converse with her about God's Word.
- Initiate prayer, journaling, and Bible verse emailing.
- Lead family worship.

Love your wife and be present with her. Your duty is to join with her in companionship. Spend time with her, talk with her, be open to having children, and then help with the children when they come. If you do not spend time with your wife, you are attacking her feelings of significance. If sports, TV, and other hobbies get more of your time and presence than she does, you are sending her the message that she is not significant to you.

One Specific Application for Husbands

As we've discussed, wives need to feel significant and secure to thrive in a marriage relationship. For this reason, husbands must remain pure through self-control. Proverbs 25:28 reads, "Like a city whose walls are broken down is a man who lacks self-control." If you lack self-control, you make yourself vulnerable to attack. If you can't say no to lesser temptations, you will not be able to resist the greater ones when they come. Then you will destroy your wife.

There are two stories in the Bible that illustrate how lust destroys a man. The first is about David when he seduced Bathsheba and killed her husband, Uriah, to conceal his adultery. The second is about David's son Amnon, a man whose "winds of 'love' proved to be nothing more than gusts of lust."[6]

2 Samuel 11:1–5,14–17

In the spring, at the time when kings go off to war, David sent Joab out with the king's men and the whole Israelite army. They destroyed the Ammonites and besieged Rabbah. But David remained in Jerusalem.

One evening David got up from his bed and walked around on the roof of the palace. From the roof he saw a woman bathing. The woman was very beautiful, and David sent someone to find out about her. The man said, "Isn't this Bathsheba, the daughter of Eliam and the wife of Uriah the Hittite?" Then David sent messengers to get her. She came to him, and he slept with her. (She had purified herself from her uncleanness.) Then she went back home. . . .

In the morning David wrote a letter to Joab and sent it with Uriah. In it he wrote, "Put Uriah in the front line where the fighting is fiercest. Then withdraw from him so he will be struck down and die."

So while Joab had the city under siege, he put Uriah at a place where he knew the strongest defenders were. When the men of the city came out and fought against Joab, some of the men in David's army fell; moreover, Uriah the Hittite died.

2 Samuel 13:1–2, 8–15

In the course of time, Amnon son of David fell in love with Tamar, the beautiful sister of Absalom son of David.

Amnon became frustrated to the point of illness on account of his sister Tamar, for she was a virgin, and it seemed impossible for him to do anything to get her....

So Tamar went to the house of her brother Amnon, who was lying down. She took some dough, kneaded it, made the bread in his sight and baked it. Then she took the pan and served him the bread, but he refused to eat.

"Send everyone out of here," Amnon said. So everyone left him. Then Amnon said to Tamar, "Bring the food here into my bedroom so I may eat from your hand." And Tamar took the bread she had prepared and brought it to her brother Amnon in his bedroom. But when she took it to him to eat, he grabbed her and said, "Come to bed with me, my sister."

"Don't, my brother!" she said to him. "Don't force me. Such a thing should not be done in Israel! Don't do this wicked thing. What about me? Where could I get rid of my disgrace? And what about you? You would be like one of the wicked fools in Israel. Please speak to the king; he will not keep me from being married to you." But he refused to listen to her, and since he was stronger than she, he raped her.

Then Amnon hated her with intense hatred. In fact, he hated her more than he had loved her. Amnon said to her, "Get up and get out!"

There are many parallels between David's sin and that of his son Amnon. Both men committed immoral acts outside marriage with beautiful women. Both men violated God's law multiple times (lusting, lying, and violence) to feed their overdosed sexual appetites. Both women experienced intense grief because of the men's adulterous actions. And both transgressions brought about death for the sons of David. Notice how Amnon hated her more than he had loved her. He fulfilled a sexual impulse, but found no love. He became hateful. God's Word is true: if you violate His commands, you will be punished by death and decay.

I remember working for an engineering company during my high school years. I worked with a number of men who built model replicas for use in testing wind pressure in huge wind tunnels. I worked there from the age of fourteen to about twenty-one. During that time, these guys worked tirelessly to keep schedules, and they produced great work. I got to see much of Boston's "Big Dig" project replicated in that wind tunnel, which was at one time the world's largest excavation project.

These were some genuinely nice guys. They were absolutely wonderful, but completely darkened at the same time. They had little self-control in speech, thought, and attitudes when it came to the beauty of women. As a young man, I couldn't even go to the bathroom without seeing naked women plastered everywhere. Naked women were at their desks, pinned up on the walls, and on their computer screen savers. These men had no idea how harmful and vulgar these things were to themselves and to others. As a young man, I watched them both love and hate women as they objectified them. As a husband and father now, I know for certain that their wives, girlfriends, or fiancées must have been hurt by their lack of self-control.

Because men are visually stimulated in virtually every way, they must protect their eyes from viewing nudity and sexuality. Films, magazines, websites, and mobile apps are targeted to men because they are a visually engaged audience group. As they watch things, they experience them as if they were actually involved. Somehow, men can enter into the fiction to such an extent that it feels real in their hearts. When they want to feel heroic, they watch a super hero on the big screen. When they want to feel strong, they play a first-person shooter game or watch sports. When they want to feel desired, they watch indecent nudity and sexuality.

The word "pornography" literally means "indecent sexual acts written down." It does not just refer to sexual images—it has an implied meaning of wrongness. The words for appropriate sex are distinct from the Greek word *porneia*, which is used exclusively to describe "indecent sex." But why is it indecent? What's the harm in making these productions or watching them? What's the harm in thinking about a woman sexually in this way?

There are three main reasons. First, the pornography industry promotes indecent treatment of women. Many sex workers are abused and exploited just to make a profit. The sex industry doesn't value women. It manipulates them. Second, actors and actresses should be pure and whole people. Any type of extra-marital sexuality is impure. Mainstream actors might think they can separate "acting" from real life, but they cannot. When they portray sexuality, they become indecent by the scene itself. It is, in and of itself, indecent to portray sexuality for others to watch.

Jesus clarifies a third problem for us when He says, "I tell you that anyone who looks at a woman lustfully has already committed adultery with her in his heart" (Matthew 5:28). By engaging in sexual thoughts through images, men attach themselves in their hearts to the women of their minds. They can have multiple women in their hearts just because they think about them seductively, and if they do this, they open their hearts to those multiple women. They create false experiences with false actions, which create false attachments and produce false expectations in the real world.

It is for this reason that this kind of thinking is sin. God doesn't want us to feed our sexual appetites outside of marriage. This is why Jesus teaches against masturbation (the eye and hand), because it leads our hearts astray. Jesus says, "If your right eye causes you to sin, gouge it out and throw it away.... And if your right hand causes you to sin, cut it off and throw it away. It is better for you to lose one part of your body than for your whole body to be thrown into hell" (Matthew 5:29-30).

A guy can show favoritism to a woman as he thinks sexually about her. He can become infatuated with a woman and obsess over her just because of the way he thinks about her. He can become angry at women in general and lash out at them because he's trained his mind that they should respond to him favorably for sex in the same way the women in his fantasies do. This can lead to terrible things such as adultery, rape, and even cases of mass murder.

Being sexually driven is a battle every man fights. I am embarrassed to say it, but I am also tempted to think of women as sexual objects. I have to actively resist this all the time. My life verse is what Paul said: "Christ came to save sinners, of whom I am the worst" (1 Timothy 1:15). Men are often adulterers in the mind. Our bentness can twist God's good intentions into a dark infatuation. However, by God's grace we can continue to find better outlets for our anxiety and testosterone fits. We can get energy out through sports and physical activities. We can have good hobbies. We *can* wait to fulfill our sexual appetite through sexual intimacy with our wife alone.

Husbands, by God's grace we must all turn away for these thoughts and images and be self-controlled. We must do this so our wives know the marriage bed is pure as we focus love exclusively on her. Thanks be to God for His grace. To Him be the glory in our homes and in the church as we sacrifice these desires.

BEAR CHILDREN AND DISCIPLE THEM

In Malachi 2:15 we read, "Has not the Lord made them one? In flesh and spirit they are his. And why one? Because he was seeking godly offspring." My church's statement of faith reads:

> God's intention for marriage is established throughout the scriptures of the Old and New Testaments; that God ordained marriage to be the voluntary union for life of one man and one woman; that sexual intimacy is legitimate only within the bounds of marriage; that this institution celebrities and compliments maleness and femaleness; and that a healthy marriage is the best foundation for families and the raising of children.

We believe this reflects the whole idea of marriage found in Scripture. Marriage is about creating homes so children can grow up in godly environments. In turn, they mature to follow God and experience His blessings through their lives. Psalm 127:1-5 states:

> Unless the LORD builds the house,
>   its builders labor in vain.
> Unless the LORD watches over the city,
>   the watchmen stand guard in vain.
> In vain you rise early
>   and stay up late,
> toiling for food to eat—
>   for he grants sleep to those he loves.
> Sons are a heritage from the LORD,
>   children a reward from him.
> Like arrows in the hands of a warrior
>   are sons born in one's youth.
> Blessed is the man
>   whose quiver is full of them.
> They will not be put to shame
>   when they contend with their enemies in the gate.

The man who trusts the Lord recognizes that children are a gift. Where secular or pagan societies see children as a nuisance, the Christian views them as a blessing of God that is not to be discarded for the pursuit of wealth or leisure. John Calvin wrote:

> As the majority of children are not always a source of joy to their parents, a second favor of God is added [in Psalm 127], which is his forming the minds of children, and adorning them with his excellent disposition, and all kinds of virtues.
>
> Aristotle in his *Politics* very properly discusses the question whether...having many children ought to be accounted among good things or no; and he decides it in the negative.... Assuredly it would [seem to him to] be a far happier lot for many to be without children, or barren, than to have a numerous offspring, proving to them only the cause of tears and groans. In order, then, to set forth this blessing of God—the having offspring—in a clear light, Solomon commends a virtuous and generous disposition in children....
>
> It is also to be added, that unless men regard their children as the gift of God, they are careless and reluctant in providing for their support.... He who thus reflects upon the goodness of God in giving him children, will readily and with a settled mind look for the continuance of God's grace; and although he may have but a small inheritance to leave them, he will not be unduly careful on that account.[7]

God has given us the joy of children. When we trust in Him to provide for our physical needs (food, shelter, work, education), we recognize the value of our children and our need to prioritize them. Instead of relying on our industry and ingenuity to thrust us into personal safety and financial security, we trust God and become faithful to the task of discipling our children. As we read in Deuteronomy 6:4-12:

> Hear, O Israel: The LORD our God, the LORD is one. Love the LORD your God with all your heart and with all your soul and with

all your strength. These commandments that I give you today are to be upon your hearts. Impress them on your children. Talk about them when you sit at home and when you walk along the road, when you lie down and when you get up. Tie them as symbols on your hands and bind them on your foreheads. Write them on the doorframes of your houses and on your gates.

When the LORD your God brings you into the land he swore to your fathers, to Abraham, Isaac and Jacob, to give you—a land with large, flourishing cities you did not build, houses filled with all kinds of good things you did not provide, wells you did not dig, and vineyards and olive groves you did not plant—then when you eat and are satisfied, be careful that you do not forget the LORD, who brought you out of Egypt, out of the land of slavery.

Do you see how God gives His people gifts they did not earn? Do you see how He provides land, houses, wells, and even vineyards and olive groves to satisfy them? As He does this, parents train their children to trust Him through life-on-life relationships. Life is the program for discipleship.

Some call this "walk along, talk along, bring along discipleship." You may have another way of describing this kind of childrearing. The point is that God has a great vision for the home. You can help your children follow Him if you remember what He has done for you and impress His commands on your children as you walk, talk, and bring them into your life and your relationship with God.

When my family went through hard times, my dad used to say, "It's going to be okay. God provides." You have already witnessed, through the pages of this book, how much my father and mother have influenced me. Even though they may have just a small inheritance to leave, they have been duly careful. I learned to trust God because my parents trusted Him.

As you men become living pictures of Christ and you women become living pictures of His church, your love for one another should overflow into a ministry to your children. And so, just as you have arrived, my dear young friends, the next generation will also arrive, because you were faithful to one another and God was faithful you to give them the inheritance of heaven.

BON VOYAGE

In the famous words of Forest Gump, another romantic comedy, "I'm not a smart man, but I know what love is."

Sometimes Hollywood gets it close, because certain stories reflect God's good intentions, but we only know what true love is because of Jesus Christ. John 15:13 reads, "Greater love has no one than this, that he lay down his life for his friends." Jesus laid down His life for us to offer us salvation and show us the most excellent way to live, that our love would be defined by His love and we would lay our lives down for our friends. We can have this love through faith. We can express this love in our youth through self-control.

We have now journeyed together through the process of courtship. All the way from check-in to arrival, my intention has been to draw our eyes to Christ so we learn what God has planned for marriage. It is now time for me to leave you to your own decisions. My prayer for you is that you will move past the romantic comedies into the wonderful deep love of Christ. I also pray that you will celebrate godly maleness and femaleness. May God richly bless you as you seek His face and acknowledge His Word. May He shine His face upon your marriage as you live out your calling to each other. May your sons be like well-nurtured plants and your daughters be like pillars carved to adorn a palace. May your children rise up to call you blessed.

Life when you're young is like walking toward a new sun rising! It's a long hike on a cold brisk morning. Life when you're young is an adventurous journey. It's flying for the first time. A little further on, though—when you've experienced the joys and sorrows of marriage, for better or for worse, with children tagging along—life is splashing at the beach in the midday sun with kids building sand castles nearby. It's joining hands with your love, sipping a glass of wine on the deck, and cuddling in the cool evening. Life when you're mature is a wise planned-out family holiday. It's being able to afford first class because you've been faithful in economy.

Bon voyage!

Connect with the author at:
www.michaelthiessen.org

Endnotes

Chapter 1: Check-in
1. Tracy Clark-Flory, "In Defense of Casual Sex," *Salon Magazine*, August 2008, accessed March 18, 2009, http://www.salon.com/2008/08/01/chastity_books/.
2. Lawrence B. Finer, "Trends in Premarital Sex in the United States, 1954–2003" *Public Health Reports* 122, no. 1 (January-February 2007): 73-78, accessed August 19, 2014, http://www.ncbi.nlm.nih.gov/pubmed/17236611
3. D.A. Carson, *The Gospel According to John, The Pillar New Testament Commentary* (Grand Rapids, MI: Inter-Varsity Press), 1991.
4. "Divorces by Province and Territories," Statistics Canada, last modified November 18, 2008, accessed November 12, 2013, http://www.statcan.gc.ca/tables-tableaux/sum-som/l01/cst01/famil02-eng.htm.

Chapter 2: Security Gate A—Truth Exists
1. J. J. Davis, *Evangelical Ethics: Issues Facing the Church Today*, third edition (Phillipsburg, NJ: Presbyterian & Reformed Pub Co., 2004), p. 4.
2. Jacques Derrida, "Structure, Sign, and Play in the Discourse of the Human Sciences," in *Writing and Difference*, trans. Alan Bass (London: Routledge, 2001), pp. 278-294. http://hydra.humanities.uci.edu/derrida/sign-play.html (accessed January 8, 2015).
3. N.T. Wright, *The New Testament and the People of God: Christian Origins and the Question of God*, vol. 1 (Minneapolis, MN: Augsburg Fortress Publishers, 1992), pp. 62-64.
4. William Gairdner, *The Trouble with Canada Still* (Toronto, ON: Key Porter Books, 2010), p. 49.

Chapter 3: Security Gate B—Trust Christ
1. Matthew Henry, *Matthew Henry's Commentary on the Whole Bible: Complete and Unabridged in One Volume* (Peabody, MA: Hendrickson, 1994), p. 244.
2. Rev. George Rawlinson, "Deuteronomy" in *The Pulpit Commentary*, ed. H.D.M. Spence-Jones (Toronto, ON: Funk & Wagnalls Company, 1909), p. 122.
3. Henry, *Matthew Henry's Commentary on the Whole Bible*, p. 244.

Chapter 4: Security Gate C—Why Friends Become Lovers
1. Larry Crabb, *The Marriage Builder* (Grand Rapids, MI: Zondervan, 1992), p. 29. Dr. Crabb makes it clear in his writings that faith in Christ is the only complete way to become significant and secure. As humans, we all have limitations. Husbands cannot dump all their needs on their wives, and wives cannot dump all their needs on their husbands. Only Christ, in His perfect life, death, and resurrection, which pays for our sin, can give us full and eternal significance and security.
2. Walt Larimore and Barb Larimore, *His Brain, Her Brain* (Grand Rapids, MI: Zondervan, 2008), pp. 38-39.
3. Ibid., p. 39.
4. Barbara Wilson, *The Invisible Bond* (Colorado Springs, CO: Multnomah Books, 2006), pp. 55-57.
5. Wilson, *Kiss Me Again: Restoring Lost Intimacy in Marriage* (Colorado Springs, CO: Multnomah Books, 2009), p. 123.
6. Mark Gungor, "Laugh Your Way to a Better Marriage" (video), Crown Studio, 2013, disc 1.
7. Dr. Douglas Rosenau, *A Celebration of Sex* (Nashville, TN: Thomas Nelson, 2002), p. 164.
8. Faithlife Corporation, "Female Friend-Sister," Logos Bible Software, Bible Sense Lexicon (Bellingham, WA: Faithlife Corporation, 2015), logos4:Senses;KeyId=ws.sister_friend.n.01.
9. John Wesley, *Song of Solomon,* electronic ed., Wesley's Notes (Albany, OR: Ages Software, 1999).

10. John Peter Lange, Philip Schaff, Otto Zockler, and W. Henry Green, *A Commentary on the Holy Scriptures: Song of Solomon* (Bellingham, WA: Logos Bible Software, 2008).

Chapter 5: Boarding and Departure
1. William Gairdner, *The Trouble with Canada Still* (Toronto, ON: Key Porter Books, 2010), p. 385.
2. Peter and Geri Scazzero use this term in *Emotionally Healthy Skills 2.0 Workbook* (Elmhurst, NY: Emotionally Healthy Spirituality, 2012), pp. 37-38.

Chapter 6: In-flight Lounging
1. J. Héring and H. Conzelmann, quoted in A.C. Thiselton, *The First Epistle to the Corinthians: A Commentary on the Greek Text*, New International Greek Testament Commentary (Grand Rapids, MI: W.B. Eerdmans, 2000), p. 594.
2. Ibid.
3. John Stott, quoted by D.L. Akin in *1, 2, 3 John* in *The New American Commentary*, vol. 38 (Nashville, TN: Broadman & Holman Publishers, 2001), p. 170.

Chapter 7: Baggage Claims
1. Donald Vassar, "When You Can't Shake, Shake, Shake It Off," The Gospel Coalition, accessed January 13, 2015, http://www.thegospelcoalition.org/article/when-you-cant-shake-shake-shake-it-off.
2. Dr. Douglas Rosenau, *A Celebration of Sex* (Nashville, TN: Thomas Nelson, 2002), p. 14.
3. Ibid., p. 17.
4. This term is taken from *The Marriage Course* by the Holy Trinity Brompton Church (London, United Kingdom). *The Alpha Marriage Course* informed the outline and vocabulary of this small section significantly. It is a valuable resource for couples.

Chapter 8: Arrival

1. Voddie Baucham, "The Truth on Marriage, Based on Ephesians Chapter 5," Youtube sermon, accessed August 24, 2014, https://www.youtube.com/watch?v=uRVD20mRAsE.
2. Ibid.
3. H.W. Hoehner, *Ephesians,* in *The Bible Knowledge Commentary: An Exposition of the Scriptures,* edited by J. F. Walvoord and R. B. Zuck (Wheaton, IL: Victor Books, 1985), Ephesians 5:22–6:9.
4. Mark Gungor, "Laugh Your Way to a Better Marriage" (video), Crown Studio, 2013, disc 1.
5. Steve Bell, "Alone Tonight," on *Romantics and Mystics,* Signpost Music, 1997.
6. R.D. Bergen, *Samuel,* in *The New American Commentary,* vol. 7:1, 2 (Nashville, TN: Broadman & Holman Publishers, 1996), p. 382.
7. J. Calvin, *Psalms,* in *Calvin's Commentaries* (Albany, OR: Ages Software, 1998), Psalm 127:3.